FOR THE
FIGHTING
SPIRIT OF THE
WALNUT

FOR THE FIGHTING SPIRIT OF THE WALNUT

TAKASHI HIRAIDE

translated from the Japanese by SAWAKO NAKAYASU

A New Directions Book

Manufactured in the United States of America
New Directions Books are printed on acid-free paper
First published as a New Directions Paperbook (NDP1099) in 2008
Published simultaneously in Canada by Penguin Books Canada Limited

Cover Design by Ann Weinstock
Interior Design by Eileen Baumgartner

Library of Congress Cataloging-in-Publication Data

Hiraide, Takashi, 1950-
    [Kurumi no sen'i no tame ni. English]
    For the fighting spirit of the walnut / Takashi Hiraide; translated from
    the Japanese by Sawako Nakayasu.
        p. cm.
    ISBN 978-0-8112-1748-4 (alk. paper)
    I. Nakayasu, Sawako   II. Title.
PL852.I663K8 2008
895.6'15—dc22
                              2008000619

New Directions Books are published for James Laughlin
by New Directions Publishing Corporation
80 Eighth Avenue, New York, NY 10011

FOR THE FIGHTING SPIRIT OF THE WALNUT

The publication of Takashi Hiraide's *For the Fighting Spirit of the Walnut* translated in its entirety into English is a thrilling event. In the twenty-something years since its original Japanese publication in 1982, this serial poem has been translated into Chinese, English, French, Russian, and other languages, but only in scattered excerpts. One of the exciting aspects of this current book – which now collects all 111 poems in English translation – is the prospect of what might emerge out of its aggregate: the contrapuntal development (and the play, multiplication, conflict) of themes, along with an envelope of orchestration which traverses multiple scales of time (of the poet, walnut, Japanese literature). One is reminded of just how big (grand, substantial, booming) the "fighting spirit" of small things such as walnuts (and insects, plums, the space between brushstrokes, a moment of eye contact) might be. Percolating out of this cacophonous and tender work, laced with an erudition that is equal parts sincere and tongue-in-cheek, are emotionally heightened turns of literary logic, and challenging exercises in style, rhetoric, and syntax. And underlying it all, throughout this utterly compassionate book, "Cheering is heard from afar" (#54) – allowing considerations of who or what this book was really written "for." Anglophone readers are now invited to open up this small but tightly packed nut of a book and begin to consider Hiraide's multifarious literary projects at both the micro- and macrocosmic levels.

...

Hiraide claims he began his life as a poet in 1964 (at age fourteen), when he wrote an elegiac homage to his two favorite mathematicians, János Bolyai and Nikolai Lobachevsky. His eighth-grade teacher surprised him by admiring the prose piece as "a great poem" – whereas he had not even realized he had written a poem at all. Twelve years later, in 1976, the publication of his first and only book of free verse, *The Inn*, garnered significant critical acclaim: Hiraide represented a new generation of Japanese poets born after the war. Following this success, his second book, *For the Fighting Sprit of the Walnut* (hereinafter abbreviated as FFSW), once again commanded great attention, as it marked a crucial, albeit early, turn in Hiraide's career, in which he begins his lifelong explorations of prose as the Idea of poetry, extended syntax, and a poetics of the grammatical line. The work, which contains many of the seeds of Hiraide's poetic thinking and ideals, placed Hiraide along a lineage of Japanese prose poetry that traces through Minoru Yoshioka back to Sakutaro Hagiwara, and he has since become one of the most respected and admired of Japan's contemporary poets. While some of his other works in prose develop more narratively, in FFSW the major themes appear in the first three sections, then subsequently develop rhizomatically, or like a musical composition: form is emergent (like fruit on a tree, the cracking of a nut, a train from the underground), rather than encompassing.

Hiraide's work strikes us as ineluctably contemporary, in part because his literary output reaches far beyond the bounds of the strictly poetic. Many of the genres and styles that interest him make an appearance in FFSW: lyric, phenomenological, faux-scientific, rhetorical, abstract, descriptive, and observational writing are blended with a playful, subtle humor. Classical diction and uses of kanji are juxtaposed or combined with present-day slang. His own poetics statements make regularly sequenced appearances. And tucked away in the folds are also traces of diary, autobiography, and even some literary feuding. Yet this book is only the beginning of Hiraide's experiments in hybrid-genre writing. His third book, *Portrait of a Young Osteopath* (1984), invents a new intersection between nature writing and poetry, while *Green Ray in My House* (1987) is written in the form of alternating free verse, prose poetry, and narrative prose. In the year 2000, following the death of his father, he published a book of tankas, *One Hundred and Eleven Tankas to Mourn My Father,* to highly controversial acclaim. In a country where the communities of contemporary poets and traditional (haiku or tanka) poets are highly segregated, Hiraide is one of the few poets to have crossed over that thick dividing line.

Other works blend poetry, essay, and autobiography – including *Notes for My Left-hand Diary* (1993), and a surreal, autobiographical novel called *A Guest Cat* (2001). *The Berlin Moment*, his 2002 travel memoir, follows the traces of Franz Kafka, Walter Benjamin and Paul Celan. *Postcards for Donald Evans* (2001), written for the American artist who hand-painted postage stamps of imaginary countries, could alternately be considered prose poetry, art criticism, epistolary fiction, or diaristic prose; *The Poetics of Baseball* (1989), true to its name, is just as much about baseball as it is about poetics. Similarly, *William Blake's Bat* (2004) collects short essays on his ordinary life, about which the novelist Natsuki Ikezawa wrote, "I would like to evade calling these writings essays or stray notes or short pieces. They are very beautiful, but the reader can't tell how this beauty was devised. They are perhaps concerned with his way of life, or at least with his way of living." And this way of living, so to speak, often casts a critical eye upon the poetic act itself: Hiraide's books of criticism include: *The Future of Shipwreck* (1982), *At the Tip of Attack* (1985), *Suspicion of Light* (1992), and *Multiple-Way Street* (2004). His more recent projects include an innovative critical biography of the Meiji-era poet Irako Seihaku, as well as the editing of Seihaku's *Collected Works*.

Hiraide himself jokingly refers to it all as sabotage: reflecting upon several decades of intense literary production, he notes that it has been twenty-some years since this "poet" has published a book of poetry. Never mind that many still consider him one of Japan's most interesting poets, and that he is the recipient of numerous prestigious literary awards for poetry and other genres. For a man who calls himself (on his website) "one who writes and erases poems in Japanese," issues not only of erasure but fragmentation, enclosure, and boundary are also of critical interest. Hiraide's poetics appear to stray away from poetry itself, which is precisely the point: in the place of poetry that seeks affirmation as poetry (as defined by the poetic community), Hiraide places value on distancing his work "from a world which takes poetic form as its premise." In response to criticism leveled at his work in the early 1990s, Hiraide wrote in *Multiple-Way Street*: "There came a point when I could no longer stand to speak about poetics with those who were unwilling to consider poetry from an external distance."

...

To unpack the original Japanese title: "fighting spirit" and "walnut" both have double meanings. *Kurumi* (胡桃), the Japanese word for "walnut," is homophonous with *kurumi* (包み), meaning "wrapping" or "enclosure." *Sen'i* (戦意), meaning "fighting spirit," is also homophonous to *sen'i* (繊維), meaning "fiber." Thus, embedded in the title: "fibers of the walnut," "fibers of the wrapping," and the "fighting spirit of the enclosure." Fibrous textures of battle are woven, threaded, confined and pried open. In the final section, however, "the walnut suffers" *(Kurumi wa kurushimu)* – not only in poetry, but also in translation: poetry *(shi –* also homophonous with "death") is inserted into the walnut *(kurumi)*, resulting in suffering *(kurushimi)*.

   In spite of his prolific output of poetics and criticism, Hiraide rarely directly discloses the secrets behind his own poetry (except when prodded by a mystified translator). However, in a recent book-length essay, he uncharacteristically explicates his own text, in this case, poem #4 from FFSW. The poem beginning, "Unaware of the arc lamp above..." quotes an aphorism from Walter Benjamin's *One-Way Street* entitled "Arc Lamp." Just as the poet who "loves without hope" imagines an instance of bestowing a "One-Way Street" to a lover he is unable to meet, Hiraide suggests likewise to the reader. The woman upon whom it is bestowed, "one day" while reading "Arc Lamp," without knowing it as such, will also be reading poem #4. And while the love remains unrequited, an invisible passageway is thus born, connecting those of distant existences, both in the past and future, in one breath. Like a miniscule, delicate time bomb set between itself and reality, an anachronism of method seeps out of the book, in a small lane opened by love.

Other anachronisms manifest themselves at the linguistic level. In contemporary usage the word *imouto* means "younger sister," but Hiraide's repeated usage of the term also accounts for its original meaning, a term of endearment for a lover or younger sister. Words such as *egui* (#49), which in current usage is mainly a teenage slang term meaning "gross," is written with a rarely used kanji character, and is here used in its original meaning, referring to a harsh, bitter sensation in the throat. The entire passage is sung by the stag beetle, and, with the exception of the kanji, is notated in katakana, a syllabary generally reserved for words of foreign origin. (In some media such as manga, the speech of robots, or foreigners speaking Japanese with an accent, is written in katakana to give the reader a sense of the phonic dissonance). Here the katakana is represented in English by the use of small caps, because of their visual similarities to katakana. On the other hand, when small caps are used in #23, it is because the original Japanese poem was written in a mix of kanji and katakana, with an anachronistic orthography.

Hiraide's range of diction travels vertically through Japanese language and literature, while his literary references just as often move laterally across geography. This might include the "disaster of writing" via Blanchot, or a multiplicitous resistance to narrative as seen in Benjamin's *Arcades Project*. Baudelaire's uneasy relationship to the urban interlaces with Ponge's pseudoscientific observations, while a Blakean sensibility reveals to us the lightning bolt within a drop of rain. Likewise Hiraide's interest in the fragmented passage draws from a long list of influences traversing place and time. He writes that he is interested in "the freedom of any fragment or part to connect to any other fragment, or to none other at all." Furthermore, in his examination of the poetic "line," Hiraide exposes the ambiguity between the line and the material concept of a brushstroke (the physical action which creates it), throwing into question our accepted systems of linguistic and poetic classification. Perhaps in relation to these considerations, Hiraide once noted that the act of setting the fragments for FFSW in their numbered order for book publication (they were first published in journals as parts of a serial poem, in a completely different order) required that he combine group theory with mathematical problem-solving.

Hiraide composed much of FFSW while he rode the train for work each day, but here the train-to-person (container-to-content) relationship is reversed: "Just then, I noticed a rusty blue rail bursting out of my chest…" (#59). The contrapuntal relationships between entry and exit, internal and external, nature and the city, are further manifested in the radiantly glowing subway, or a tree pushing its way into its hometown tide. Epic struggles of love and war are cast at walnut-scale: acts of violence are enacted upon the hard shell of a snail, a rotting plum, the poetic line as it is shattered into fragments. Hiraide, ever the baseball fiend, thus loads up the poetic bases – while the ball comes wafting in like a corpse candle, and a "hit" occurs as a moment of eye contact between strangers. One waits, alert, in the outfields or in an emergency reservoir of water: "And so it was that the young minnow leaps, quick, have a fire!" (#92) In linked fragments that contort the desperate pinings of a love poem, a rescue fantasy, a desired state of emergency, this moment known as the present is amplified – or, perhaps, exploded.

...

My first thanks goes to Eric Selland, who through his wonderful translations introduced me to Hiraide's work, and whose generous mentorship and knowledge of Japanese poetry have been an invaluable resource, in this project as well as others. For their help in the translation process, I would also like to thank Yu Nakai at the Yotsuya Art Studium, and Takashi Hiraide himself. They have both been incredibly generous with their patience, responsiveness, corrections, suggestions, and insights.

I thank Keith Waldrop for the only formal training I have had in literary translation; Tracy Grinnell for the *Aufgabe* assignment to edit a Japan-feature on contemporary poetry; and Jerrold Shiroma for making a lively space for translation on Duration Press. The following people have also provided encouragement, inspiration, and assistance, explicitly or by example: Benjamin Basan, Norma Cole, Forrest Gander, Jen Hofer, Rachel Levitsky, David Perry, Laura Sims, Rosmarie Waldrop. Thanks to Anne Weinstock and Eileen Baumgartner for their adept handling of the bilingual book design, and lastly, a big thanks to Jeffrey Yang and Barbara Epler for all their gracious support, enthusiasm, and hard work on the production and publication of this book.

Thanks also to those who provided material support during the translation of this book: in the form of a grant, the PEN Translation Fund; and in the form of shelter, Shigeru Kobayashi, Bard College, and Eugene Kang. The following publications have published earlier versions and excerpts of this work: *Aufgabe, Calque, Canarium, Circumference, Factorial, The Literary Review, Octopus, Poetry,* and *Versal.* Many thanks go out to the editors for their kind support.

I would also like to thank my family, now including Eugene, whose constant love and support translate to almost every facet of my life and work.

SAWAKO NAKAYASU

The radiant subway. The wall that clears up, endless. A thundering prayer of steel 1. that fastens together the days, a brush of cloud hanging upon it, O beginning, it is there – your nest.

The sound of the bursting flesh of fruit scatters between your ears. The forefront of 2. this spray beckons to those outside of sorrow.

3.   Things that rain, and things that grow. They are all that hold my interest. (Until the things that rain have grown, and the things that grow have poured.) Things that grow, and things that rain. They are all that I desire. (Until the things that grow cease to grow, and the things that rain no longer rain a single drop.)

4.   Unaware of the arc lamp above, she reads intently one day – "The one who loves without hope is the only one who knows that person."

Along the coast lined with warehouses, you were born in a pool of light. With the almond eyes you inherited from the straits. Tidal hair connecting the islands. Your burning cheeks. Soft legs that trip up at times. Though forced to fight in one place after another, because you harbor a resistance to death inside the skill with which you keep your voice down, your age slowly comes to rest upon the backsides of days.

In the wind-whirled grass, blend yourself in with the soft tear of the decayed rice paper or freshly unearthed beak. Break your bones, open your skin, and strive to get the inerasable grease, entangled and rippling up – to finally rise from the lips, toward the grass-tips, to bleed apart in scatters.

7.   Protected by a hard shell, the fight just to continue sleeping. Not only for those pitiful drupes, but also the bold army of snails who spiral single file down the escape well of a skyscraper – single-mindedly, dragging along the breath of their sleep.

8.   Continuous thoughts of packaging ice. No matter what I write it melts, even the address. If and when it arrives, that person will be gone.

The road that lightly makes herself up with frost needles, for the clamorous shoe-bottom stars: my sister. Once furrowed, she comes through the looking-glass door, resisting the spread of her own hair, and throws all her efforts into getting up. What a beast prowling the underworld would look up at, the "crazed moon."

First of all, here we do not know who sees through the interior. Upon this solid skin, inward gazes are hatched without lull, and those youthful yet deeply carved wrinkles render the skin of that sculpture called the exterior more distinct than daybreak. They frolic the way the water's edge cleaves, and coagulate, and wrap, will wrap, endlessly, all of the ocean lost to those approaching, and the comets that fall there.

11. The final puzzle regarding the shape of a poem dwells in the word 'line.' Dividing lines, changing lines. Straddling lines, crossing lines. As a line is followed, the chain of lines falls to pieces. The 'line' is neither a path, nor a discipline that closes the circle. What it is, is the shadow of a fragment. A place lacking something twice over. Speak, O seams by the name of brushstroke, the line midway – and the line space – of the line. Or is this perhaps an Archimedes' screw? Eating death, the deed grows thin.

12. An axe is flung down in the cabin of my habits and disappears. Laughing, then writing, I told someone nearby that the tongue is made of grains of blood. O you who awaken with one eye in the slits of the wooden door, good morning. And good night now. And anyway this is the street where the nearby branches grab us by the collar. Crying in the distance is a longing, addressed casually by everyone. The asphalt sheets are already gathering the wrinkles of the evening.

The strange insect called *scarabaeus* skillfully constructs round pellets from the dung of hoofed animals such as sheep, cows, and horses, and takes them to an appropriate place to be slowly consumed. For its larvae, special pellets are made by selecting only the dung of sheep, which has the most nutritional value and is easiest to digest. First the mother carefully selects the ingredients, then crushes them finely, carrying it to an underground nest. There, beginning her operation in earnest, she creates a beautiful pear-shaped pellet, and through the small hole she has left open until the very end, pushes an egg into the center. When the larva is finally hatched from the egg, it finds itself in the middle of this enormous lump of dung, and peacefully eating its surroundings, little by little grows larger.

14. Today, with a triple hangover, I slowly pedaled and pedaled my wobbly bicycle, like a mist, past a back alley that murmurs condolences.

15. From above the west-northwest cliff, an old mixing machine looks down upon the ruins of acrylic resin which, surrounded by fog, still operate with precision. The mixer stirs up memories of the few things that might have remained unscathed from itself. Honey bees, a burnt rice paddle, a broken compass needle, water at the bottom of the thermometer shelter, a woman's tongue, fire. His job is done. And finally now, those memories are transferring themselves over into our hands.

To the world from which you keep straying, you are an all-the-more refreshing fruit of gratitude. The early summer teeth of the beasts graze the inside of the room meant to be shaken by relentless sleep, and at times the rusty valley water of the metropolis traverses it as well. In the old, warped mirror that opens the night as a window, a silent fruit from the beginning, a seasonless snow from the end, falls likewise lightly upon your shoulder and yet you do not notice, do not get hurt. This fact, without touching me, encourages me. It satisfies me with the juice of a gratitude that passes by without need for a recipient. Even knowing that in due time the door will kick out these illusions along with itself, into the dust-prone morning of young foliage.

17. The radiant subway again. Today, too, in this still-radiant subway, small white explosions occur here and there. They are the sounds of our joints popping, the sound of an all-too-convenient despair fading away. The walls collapse, and the birds of the earth, now without hesitation, begin transporting their nests so as to set them into these daily-renewed explosions.

18. May the hairy danger always keep holding your hand. May the wicked prayers and select anxieties always move my lungs. And may the days not run by, the sound of love nearly escape confirmation, and the bone ash of our repeatedly burning stories cook our deeds in the furnace of destruction's truth.

If those who are denied are given even a handful of the ashes of glory, let's throw that 19. out as well. In order to honor her unclouded sorrow. The unborn words washed in anguish simply continue merrily along this shore.

The rounded back of that lonesome wrecking professional, I wonder if it isn't there, 20. the true figure of a line of poetry. Hiding his true face further within the dust that sprays back like an enemy's blood, enjoying the intensifying, post-destruction sunshine as if the damage were his own – that narrow back.

21. A faithless recognition that leaves no trace, of the dream rail that noisily burns the darkness toward your chest. Its tongue sweeps away even the falling branches of oxygen, and does not go pale, even to the single breath of driving rain that attacks from up ahead. Much less without hindrance, in spite of the apocalypse of red and yellow.

22. It is now time to describe, toward a mossy nothingness, the shape of a fragment. The moment a shipwreck seeks – against its will – the pretense of wings, and when the eraser under the eaves just about to disappear first faces itself, and when this too is nothing more than a short-lived illusion. The dim brilliance of the fragment criticizes the sharpness of the form. I follow the contours of the blade. Not for purposes of sketching, but in order to draw up a contract with the sweat of things at the moment the line tears, and to cross over to the next shape.

"BECAUSE ALL THEORIES ARE IMPLICATIONS SLIGHTLY TOO LARGE FOR THEIR SUBSTANCE, THEY SHOULD, WITH NEITHER REJECTION NOR ENCOURAGEMENT, BE RUBBED WITH CARE AND SINCERITY, SPAT UPON AS THE TRANSFERRED IMAGE SPAT OUT BY THE WAYSIDE IN BYGONE DAYS. IN THIS WAY, THY LOST, SOFT SKIN, RATHER THAN THE DRAWING, COMES TO BE DRAWN IN THIS MOVEMENT OF THE RUBBING FINGERS. SUBSEQUENTLY IT IS TO BE HIT BY A STONE, DRIED BY THE SUN, AND IF THOU SHOULDST SCRAPE AT IT ROUGHLY WITH SHARPENED FINGERNAILS OR A HIGONOKAMI KNIFE, EVEN THE DUST OF IMPLICATION SHALL APPEAR TO DANCE A SMALL TEMPEST — AND THAT IS AN ESPECIALLY JOYFUL THING."

Kafukafu, says the dutiful crow circling around my skull. Crow, O crow, in the shallow forest of, Sendagaya, kind and warmhearted Jungle Crow. O antagonistic friend.

25.   Getting off the train, there was only one exit to the north. I passed a quiet old commercial strip along the tracks, what seemed like a row of repeating liquor stores, grocery stores, and rice shops – in other words I took a long detour south around the station house. With someone leading the way, I was finally able to stand before the tree of my dreams.

26.   The soap that transforms in the hand of silence into a living thing. The railway where the claw marks of those approaching death lather fragrantly upon our skin.

No matter who might see this as reprieve, for me it grows increasingly painful. I open vertically the back of my right hand, and call in a salty, weathered, secondhand climate. The kind that crumbles at its edges with the ocean. And then with a fibrous blade of grass, I tie up my blood vessel.

I walk along the clear patch of sun that is still too cold for batting. Nevertheless, on the riverbed, the young boys shouting and pelting the abandoned car with stones.

29. The swirling has started after all. Just look at that keel tip, wavering at the directive approaching from up ahead. Just try looking through that empty memory of yours. Tied together, the bells which report their whereabouts dance, and between these dancing bells, look, the swirling has started after all.

30. The blood plasma seeping into the pavement. Sturdy arms that squeeze tight. The murky light of the city quietly pins me down, thrashes me, breaks me apart. I am a construction site in July, spreading upon a hazy brow. I lash out. Into the rumpled interval of sun. At the someone in the center. Tears belonging to no one well up, and wash, as if hitting, the pit of my stomach, sunken into the pavement.

We are running low on things to bat. Go to bat. Hold the timber vertically, thrust it slowly toward heaven (dizzying over the blue), then quietly lower it to chest level, relax, and brace yourself. A single whiff of lightning will descend through the grain of wood. From across the field, a fist-sized corpse candle comes burning in a loose curve. Give, for an instant, and bat. We are running low on things to bat. Go to bat.

Why not use your fluttering tongue to wipe the sweat off of that starling who is trying to strip off her wings. It's so distant of you, my arboreal lover on the outskirts of town. From the shadow of the clothes hanging in a thrift shop, a single antelope watches you. Steel-colored eyes of contempt.

33. Révolution . . . the inn today is a limitless organ. I interrupt it, that frugal canon. I suppress it, that F-sharp running away, the still-sunken tie. I re-dismantle the melodies over which I reign. I refracture my own self trembling from the rhythms I subjugate. Afterward I re-regulate, with the last of my one hundred and eleven deceptive cadences, the suppression the interruption the dismantling the fracturing. Why? I, too, am a scrap of strength. Because I am merely the authority of matter. Other scraps will touch upon this too, I imagine.

34. A shipwrecked light. Opening your cracked lips still wider, you call in the rusty-haired ocean. Even as you ride into the city of devotion composed only of ephemera and horizon, on the breath of a black horse in January. Your heart crushed upon the seven seas, and space, torn apart in a flash, as the fabric of water. A person now is a breach of the moment – lacking that which responds, is nothing but a distant shadow. But look – O twisted edge of shipwrecked light. The sight of the tendons in your heel, with grains of sand on them, beginning to withstand the pale constrictions of your leaps. Amidst the rising scent of grass, of thrashing, of disdain.

"Up ahead, difficulty."   35.

A late-summer greeting. Even the summer vacation spent battling the parasitic plants   36.
has passed away, just barely in time. Because at the windowsill the imagination can't
help but move beyond and toward the future of words, I rest my chin upon my arm,
with which I strike at the jealousy of imagination. The city's emotions, too, are
nothing but the pulse of language. I have sent an early-decaying leaf. And so then,
until the sacrifice of your madness.

37.   The meshed pathway that once was made to run, capriciously, by the fresh, juicy fibers of fruit – now, as it is, comes to cover its entirety with a hardness like never before – ring this perfect bell. In this underpass of ours that forbids open flames, ring this utterly exposed labyrinth. At first, it does not ring. At first, it does not ring.

38.   Hey, say it again, one more time. Come see how the dust rises when you say it again, right here, hey you, say it again.

Taking the thinness of the edges as subject, to assess the shape of what remains unfulfilled. For example, the scab of wind beginning to shroud my remains. The music of a desire toward birth that never learns its lesson – coming and going through those fragile cells, making them breathe.

To trace the rooftop ridges of a backlit city, drinking the spring water at the point of cohesion. Entering the room, a pulse is taken right when the heart is crushed upon a color-printed newspaper. And so it is that today, too, a line of poetry goes without shooting you, and is nothing more than a soundless watery segment floating up for the first time, finally, enfolded in the gathering dusk of a long detour. However, to proceed while towing the emotions of the extremely low-speed bullets – along the road with the dim radiance of an intestinal wall – must be none other than an exceptional tribulation.

41.   Holding fast to the dappled mane of the drill-worn cape, into a night of winter waves, I crossed a flowing threshold. The day sunk, the lighthouse fell still darker into sleep, and over the entire ocean the wind blew itself to tin. Already too late, crouched over the prow of the ground as it sidled toward the ocean, the ocean, I saw it – through its interior the sea-rusted subway thundering along, straighter than a gaze. And at the very end, my dead people, wearing green starfish on their backs . . .

42.   As the outbreak of ideas is pushed to zero, there is a white explosion. I am inclined to call this, and only this, poetry. Beneath the cupola under a precipice, I was bathed numerous times in so much misfortune as would get lost in the rays of the sun. While one after another, the fruits of rain grow on my head.

The spider is genius. The celerity that moves, leading the air mass, the atmospheric level that falls higher than the clouds connecting the seasons. The spider is genius. The brilliance descending in sixteen directions is not a gravity-evading parachute, but striates the entire sky, guiding drops of light to the ground. And it lowers itself, while it's at it. How can bones be so transparent – bones that flood over, even as they break. And plus, it is a seed. With endurance and imagination as nourishment, the scheme is rather null. Sorcery is rather null. A light-handed evil that admits no glory, not even its own. The spider is simply genius. 43.

Verse finds strength in being segmented. Dependent on neither future nor past, it persistently dangles between line space and line space. Like a child who cries all alone in the dark for a long time, it tries to tear itself as far away as possible from the shadows of time. Moreover, they are the ones that are, through segmentation, placed into lines. 44.

45.   I broke my favorite black bat on the light descending to the inside angle. At that, the Tokyo Bay Landfill Number 13 Baseball Grounds (Small) began effacing the grass surrounding the softly glowing left-handed batter's box, as the crest of a wave quivered toward me, like a whisper. Oh that's just fine. Keep laughing forever. At this bare-handed batter with neither age nor regret, beginning to collect like an unraveled raft the broken ends I used to gaze upon, into the space of memory.

46.   Lost amidst the trees in the ripening orchard, longing – commensurate with my shoddy scheming – grew thick before us in the form of leaves chewed off by bugs; conversely, his withered hostility seemed to be closing in upon my body, firmly yet unguardedly.

Admitting to a beautiful shadow outside itself, the creature is wounded, around the chest. Its moss-grown hand still twitches in space, outstretched in an attempt to touch, fearful of losing. Nevertheless, it needs to announce, though lacking the voice with which to announce. That its breath has become a small storm. Staking the downfall of this creature upon what is held dear.

47.

The work of discovering numerous cul-de-sacs. Patiently walking, out in the field. As soon as I find one, I tie up its mouth. In a secret corner of the city, doing nothing at all but waiting for a pinhole just wide enough to let a breath through, to develop between two sacks. Rupture – Concatenation. Then, all that is left is the breezy task of walking along, undoing the strings.

48.

49. Beside a parking lot at dusk, in a small excuse of a bush, a stag beetle sings silently: "MY WAY OF LOVING IS INFERIOR TO THAT OF THE *CLICK BEETLE*. MY STRIDE IS NOTHING COMPARED TO THAT OF THE *ELEPHANT BEETLE*. THIS SINGING VOICE, TOO, IS FAR OFF-KEY COMPARED TO THE *ROVE BEETLE*. BUT STILL, I CHEW BITTER STEMS AND FLY ABOUT EVERYWHERE. THIS IS BECAUSE I BELIEVE IN THE ERROR OF *SHE* WHO WILL ONE DAY BE FORCED TO APPROVE OF MY EXISTENCE."

50. You who crawl past on the breath of an insect, along the unowned floor as it is suspended – I am your breath. Here and there, as the snow crumbles off the tree branches one after another, and when a ray of light pours vertically in, it is my moment. Let's set out in pursuit of that pristine crime of the bicycle grinding over the ice on the road and leaving this place.

Despite any kind of a poetics of rejection, it is impossible to conceal the joy of those 51. who sympathize through metaphor. A single particle of white clover pollen digging into the northern wall near the rooftop of a skyscraper is a modest rhetorical view, visible to those who wish to view it. You should go read those exchanges between those who are repeatedly pounded by sunshowers. Beginning with "Denying the Reader," all the way up to that tall, tall, love scene.

A bad habit of calling upon comets from the darkness of a taxicab. Yes, turn left at 52. the dead light up ahead, crank the wheel completely to the right, skimming the window of the clock store at the end of the street. Soon, dragging only the tail – downward. To the radiant subway.

53. The wind passes through the train car, the sunny spot on the blue seat holds still, and I am on my way to see someone who struggles on the brink of death. For part of the way, I exchange playful glances with a kind something that I encountered; then I get up, leave, and walk alongside the wind to the back of the train. Oh, I lose my sense of which direction we are moving in. The verdurous capital that opens up in the last window. O, final window – will I be returning here once again, with even just a smile, from the hospital.

54. Midway down the deep darkness of the trash bin, the kid plum finally caught on. "Oh, I am about to rot away, without ever having leapt, never having known anything tough and shiny." And then, through the wet wrappers and bread crumbs, he slid down two plum-lengths. Cheering is heard from afar.

I come from that primary fiction created by words holding each others' hands. I am the 55.
one who trims stories down into the smallest possible pieces, the one who walks along
clipping off the fingers of entangled words with a single line of revenge. This walk,
unbeknownst to people, has neither outlook, nor return, nor any kind of compassion.

Your arm has become a twisted rail, rusted and stretched out. On the slope of your 56.
side, a single seed of grass has been run over and squashed. Your heel is wounded,
overflowing with white smoke. I can't save you. From the backs of your knees, a
white smoke billows terribly upward.

57.   Spirits wrapped in a skin of green. On each one, lushly growing, a hanging drop of thunderstorm!

58.   When that shadow was with me, I felt like I could part the curtain of mist and walk on and on endlessly toward the dangerous side. The bitumen flowers were already disheveled and fallen, and anything you could call a fence was sodden and shivering. When I pulled my finger out of my chest, I ventured to take that hand, and then the two of us tried to meaninglessly fling ourselves, fluttering, into space. A flash of light had denied all our leaps, however – even faster than the sound of the fruits of rain hitting the ground, those which had earlier begun to fall.

Just then, I noticed a single rusty blue rail bursting out of my chest, falling to the
asphalt in front of me. I dropped to my knees in time with the landing, and it sped
up, stretched even further, and was pulled into the underground stairs before me, which
seemed to be cradled quietly in the belly of a lonely, faint black stone architecture.
I crawled forward while drawing the track back into my chest, until I finally arrived
at the entrance, and peeked in. Far beyond the cavity made of bones, near two
intersecting beams of light, something with a dim shadow. And then, something
surging forth from who knows when.

Such an unnatural itinerary (gradation) between the banners of reality and realization.
Action's lodging is swallowed by a completely weakened grass fire, and the groan
beginning to escape takes action. The paltry wingbeat and the stillness finally both
belong to us. He who is unable to wear – on the backside of his own voice – this
reality of a fly that hovers around like a punctuation mark is, between one aspect and
another, a pickpocket already pounded to pieces.

61.   On the blackboard in my elementary school, a patched-up wing, pinned with nails. A half-cooked sunset printed out from the rotary press. Pushing apart the shiny, yielding limbs of my classmates, heeding only the silent teachings of minerals, kicking through the window of the specimen room in the riverbed – I have graduated – O fragile night of the moon – all alone, holding a single hard eraser.

62.   When the typhoon approached, clamping down the dying summer, and the waves washed the small house on the embankment, the light was cut off and Teruzō – the disgruntled Irako Seihaku shining the sharp circle of his flashlight on a gulf on the map taped to the ceiling of his study – having abandoned his boat to the silence and retired in his old age to a sea village, suddenly became joyful, saying, "The wind will change at any moment," and "Continue north or turn to the right" – with two books of meteorological studies by his side, it is said that he was filled with feverish excitement, and faltered, was moved. *That* small boat.

When I read the yellowing civil notice regarding the traces of the strange small animal who splits walnuts cleanly in two, it was the same clear afternoon that I had received a very brief note from the woman with long black hair who rode an old train cutting through groves of walnut trees in full blossom back to her homeland to visit someone dying, but with its arrival, that yellow-green postcard split the dusk of my day's cabin cleanly in two.

The gaze is easily caught because it is too long. It pours into the beady round lake and causes a great spray. And without a moment's pause gets entangled with the gaze that turns back and connects the spray. As a street will intersect another street, they sympathize to the point of losing the distinction between self and other. For the winter of hatred, the evening of contempt, even for the morning on the hill of resolute rejection. The thread of the all-too-long significance unravels and the open sea of the swoon spreads, in blue. One who looks into a single pair of eyes has already drowned in all of the waters.

65. What I constantly correspond with is the arm in the prism tied up in a tall canopy of trees. A rainbow that smolders near the elbow. Words seem to arrive, from no matter how microscopic the creature. Moreover, they extend into the burning mobile, the abundant growth between the trees beat upon by day. On a distant roadside, using the sour water of experience, I, too, assemble an impoverished shadow.

66. And so again, verse is a shattered dominance. Nerves that continue to get by through their avoidance of such matters should just leave behind this precipice of thin ink. Fragments will no doubt cut the hands that touch them.

Clutching my bag stuffed with fragments, I buy a box of Morinaga milk caramels, 67.
and the Sobu-Chuo local train crosses the capital city high in the sky, east to west.
Here is my workroom. Human speech fades and swells at each station, and by the
time the train turns back, around Tsudanuma, the soles of my shoes have grown
rough. The winter darkness, as if in invitation, turns clear blue, and my meandering
gaze also begins its clunky return from the far reaches of the paper. Rub your eyes.
With all the windows and doors and straps (and even wire racks), where the bells
ring and the whistle blows, this is the workroom of the dead signal engineer child.

Having passed through numerous summers, one poet wrote the following – "Why 68.
should it be   that I would learn   from what I have lost." In the darkness of
the penetrating cold, beside the train tracks, still aslant from a severe intoxication and
hoping at least for the day to end, I find myself connecting strange thoughts – could
I now learn, from what I am losing.

69. (Even as I roll about here, I have never for a moment forgotten about the loving, large head of Guillaume Albert Vladimir Alexandre Apollinairis de Kostrowitzky, injured by a shell and wrapped up in bandages.)

70. Won't you throw one for me, O Ms. Hare, resting upon a beam by the first murmurings of the brook, when a pulverized verse is your only weapon, from there, just one word . . . . . . and then, "a hit." The sound scatters upon the moldy aluminum foil.

The reason you gave up chasing the crumbling weather based on the forecast is 71. because you, too, are a living creature, I think. You issue forth out of the grass, fill the air like bird lice in spring, seek some warmth on a tree bark, and wilt away. A rotten smell will ensue. From the tree's underflow to the sewage line, logic splits off and the figure spills. However,

Really, after coming so far. We're pretty horrible, aren't we. You can't even read as 72. much as has been written. You can't even write as much as will be read. A refractive index that lightly possesses all in this world that is paper, all that is meat. A letter to the mirror, a tin journal . . . . . . the one single name erased repeatedly on the wave. Despair? Nah. Using the horizon as a bookmark, I only close the blue sky in here.

73. Emerging from the hole where the praying mantis dies, the theoretical questions had already come to an end. Making our campsite around the shadow of the wind, from here let's say we gaze upon hope and pomegranate decay, and the clandestine meeting between the pomegranate and the muzzle, together as one concatenation. Until each moment observed becomes the bone structure of the wind, and the wind, unaware, grabs its own neck, shaking and blowing on it.

74. Floods and echoes conclude by being sucked into the urethane and then the sewer. Intermittent piano music from a distant window, the rustling of a young Zelkova tree near the window. They, too, will eventually come to their end, sucked into the burning eardrum. O no-longer-visible-person-swallowed-by-the-crowds – I am well. With no floods nor echoes, I am extremely well.

Stardust, Sun, Saturn, Lightning. It is not merely a matter of being corrupted by white 75. and orange numbers and symbols. According to one point of view, the road is universe-like, abounding in sexy patches. Gas, water, phone, electricity, police. Police? I have been seeing less and less of the rabbit poking only its ears up out of the manhole.

Easily boarding the train after withstanding hopes to hollow out its body, the tree visits 76. the tree itself. It pushes its way into its hometown tide, following, like the tail of an animal, the wilted, grain-like city drooping into the ocean. Sure, the error was a known fact. O father, on the leaf tip. All words are *drupes of the after-flower*.

77. I have been organizing fragments for a long time now. Individual cul-de-sacs filling a tote bag are each driven into a form with much less leeway, and before they manage to connect with one another, are left in the hands of yet another display-belt of chance. The longer this work continues, more hands that cross over from one fragment to another change into an intermediate term equivalent to a fragment.

78. Squirrels are, namely, tree squirrels. They also come to the ground, but for the most part they traipse among the treetops, damaging the vegetation. There are few nuts that squirrels do not eat. In particular, beechnuts, acorns, and walnuts are some of my very favorites.

Clutched tightly in the bosom of the enemy, what sort of love letter or declaration or will could there be at this point. We are all unexploded shells, wrapped around an inner field of nettles. Partitions that lack each others' separated beloved. Wrinkled eyes reflect on the cellophane cleft hanging from my shoulder. Things that will break, for certain, at a precise cross section. It is now time for me to part ways with these guys, right through that cross section.

O son of mine – in neither a drawer of memories nor a coffin of the future – listen. Like an instrument abandoned on the street, the edges of your mouth cracked, even your pattern pointlessly grazed, there is nothing left for you but to muster up a feeble wind in a small tree hollow, tremble at your own strength, and keep growing clearer. Aside from encouraging a single cowering snippet and being comforted by a single passing snippet, and thus supporting yourself on the melody that weaves itself together, and then changing yourself according to the fearful trembling that arrives on its own, now, at last, there seem to be no other means.

81. Railroad crossing guard, look at the sky where the leaf mulch spreads. Slowly raise one arm, just now expended from ringing, for the withered bolt of lightning randomly passing by, the bone structure of the mole, the illusions of the seasick. Keep your asbestos hat deep on your head. The underground standby is eventually filled with the signal of betrayal.

82. I turn the sodden, warped corner of the osteopathy clinic, indeed I turn it. The wind changes to blue serum, trembles but does not blow, and blocks of clouds expand, then shrink. My fingers open, indiscreetly upon my boiling chest. Yeah, they open indiscreetly.

One day, in the afternoon after the rain, on the escalator going from the west side of
the first floor to the second floor of the Takashimaya store in Nihonbashi, I saw a
single snail in front of me, and found myself sighing deeply at the pointlessness of his
rhyme. Would he now proceed to the greenery on the rooftop, or head straight to the
kitchen of the main dining hall. Or perhaps he has some shopping to do. At least get
yourself up to the magic section, little spiral. I whispered words of encouragement,
but all I saw was maybe a shy little twitch of the tentacles.

An exacting room protected only by a distant resonance. There, introspection and
bewilderment——*Juglans*——bewilderment and prayer——*Juglandaceae*——there is no
salvation even in considering oneself a small animal.

85.   A hesitancy toward living, under the resist-dyed "Chinese" sign in the outlying quarters. Reflected in the glass in front of the food displays, the throngs of people waver. Brought together by chance, each placed on an imaginary scale: the true essence of that which is comforting, and that which comforts. In *that* kind of posthumous dusk.

86.   Poetry has continued to differ way too much from what people believe it to be. Yes, that must be it, and just now as I think this, a shelf in the bar tilts.

The movement in my fingertips – all the finer, beclouded – as I crush a winged ant. 87.
The dark cloud of handwriting that gushes forth as I erase a mistake, all the thicker
and messier. When I die, I wonder what kind of bird will descend on my chest from
between the real clouds, leaving what kinds of deranged scratch marks, pecking at
my feeble spirit.

If a work can stave off the strife of the world's disasters, and simultaneously wrap 88.
this disaster in as the oxygen of its own world, then the gaps between words,
seemingly hand in hand, between those breaths, one slightest hint and another, is the
very basis of its solidity. And relaying through these vacant holes, the work is reversed
back to the world. And so then we possess the ultimate right to read in any order
each air hole in the work while overriding the time of the writing – the right to
exercise the final disaster, so to speak, of the work.

89. The spirit that gets run over and torn apart by what it holds most dear. But just as the disseverance accepted this as the reason for its disseverance, he could have been waiting for it. His own carcass. The scattering. I believe I really saw this – the walnut intently nodding this way, trembling in the final rumbling.

90. Concrete blocks with grass, flying about in the spread of cooled eyes. On each of the one thousand coffins blanketing the canal in a row, still one thousand more cooled eyes. The brigade of baby fog-particles racing down the hanging bluff. The boundless reflex knitting together the death-ruined city with one sweep. Only in such dazzle can I use up my secret art and, O sister, forever and whenever, hold you in your absence.

The young rustling breeze blowing through the trees of a borrowed landscape, beside   91.
the glass window, insists it is a migratory anticyclone. The cheerful hustler. In this
spring of brute strength, you've tired yourself out confirming the balance between
the fading halo and the boiling light. I, too, am to quickly understand, from that
hoarse voice of yours, that something boiling over inside me has expended the
balance of noon.

And so it was that the young minnow leaps in the emergency reservoir. And so it was   92.
that he leaps, quick, have a fire!

93. In the funerary sculpture of the ancient Egyptian scribe believed to be called Kai, the traditional pose in which he is seated, with papyrus in his left palm and his chest puffed out, beyond indicating, himself all ears and hands, that it was a warning to heed all the logic and changes of the Pharaoh's dictates, was also an oblivion filled with pride for his first-class occupation, this occupation beyond occupations. But today, (what is believed to be) the reed pen in the right hand has been lost, and in each area a little bit of damage, and a museum-like bliss, has seeped in.

94. With our blind eyes and ringing ears, *Juglans*, let us turn the corner at the end of this ravaged time. In the omen of couplings and floodings, *Juglans*, let us throw out our chests, and throw them out again, and raise our voices to their roughest extent, descending the stairs at the end of these desolate days. The seasons have been torn apart. And then the clouds, the waves, filling the earth madly, though with shyness, *Juglans*, a radiant, false after-death begins to slowly move through our underground.

The battle of poetic forms, like a rag tossed on the pavement, is wet with recently   95.
spilled stars. What passes above it is a mechanism simply for passing by, a glance to
be ignored. The formulaic camp remains blind to this section where such scenery
emerges, but wrapped inside an old rallying call is rather a single section of acropathy
patients eager to capsize the encircling cobblestones through the freedom of poetic form.
They close their small eyes to the fact that a form of free verse is already a form at
the disposal of political power, and that a rag waves no differently from a nation's flag.

Only a satisfying hit teaches me the way of sorrow, and only a trenchant light comes   96.
to console my crushed heart. And every single grain in a spray of dirt shudders for the
long-awaited end. Perhaps I should overturn this place, along with my appreciation,
back to the perfectly clear sky.

97.   Walnut, you'll have a hell of a time there. Why go to such a place, drenched in black sweat? Walnut, I am closing in on you. Can't you hear it, the rumble of my steel?

98.   The bliss of existing after having been erased. Crushed and in that form, the joy of bathing in the first light. Traces of the sprinkling will sizzle madly in the zero-degree fire – the force of crystallization into the force of destruction, and the force of destruction into the clatter of what is destroyed, are now struck back into the course of the swirl I've just lived through.

A train whose one hundred and eleven cars each simultaneously break into the lead
past the thin hazy air of the midnight sun. Their linking is discretionary. A train
whose one hundred and eleven cars each trail the withered scenery behind their
backs. Dissection is voluntary. Upon what kind of track would such a train run, O
train, lease this illusory space, and graph it.

Summoning up my very last bit of energy, I shall bring a few gifts to your pale
doorway. So they might become your first bit of food before heading over to the
other eye. Whirling tides that are sealed in. And the sun with new bandages. Drupes
with wisdom.

101. The coldness of the water of mayhem, swaying in the just-broken jug. Blessed by misfortune, we part ways. As the rivers did, long ago. As humans did, long ago. The tired wind is better off still more tired, and the faded bushes are better off still more faded. The shrunken spirits should simply scatter, like so many bits of gravel. One day – under the decaying tree that suddenly buds – enemies, lovers, all will come to bitterly know who owns this very special misfortune that I bless.

102. Little sister. A common-law bolt of lightning, scattered clouds that move through the underpass. A distant fire deep in the heart, a keyhole made of light. The most impassive, most scathing, pearl.

Wrapped inside the palm of my hand, the water ripens. But the water does not crumble – is it because of the flower inside, twisting itself. Strength fades; beauty, too, must only be a condition. Without gazing, without drinking it down, like a high tower, like the green mane of the high tower that day, I would like to stand myself up on the bottom of an echoless love. I would like to make myself trail in the wind, thrown into the dead faint of drowning. Harming the gulf without a coast.

The window was always a mirror that gazed out onto a small graveyard. Everyone has those days when they do nothing but furrow, there, with a vague stare. Of course, I too once had a single room on the second floor of a wooden house flanked by a vague iron handrail.

105. The poetic methods of the fog descending the stairs finally connect the snake to the melody, love having been thus fulfilled in the heart. They make the already-disclosed sacrament, and one ignorant, fluttering wagtail, come to terms on the backside of hope. From the sheer edge of the throat's wall, the ultramarine rust spills over onto the white paper, as if to dance. My shadow once again stands upon the underground where the withered bones of words consumed with love thinly grow, though it is no longer quite so, that this is a keyhole to whatever kind of field.

106. What a great number of mistakes, without being known as such, lap up against us every day. Along with the signals welling up in bitter waves is a gradually understood lesson. However, in the shadow, an increasingly suspicious truth.

We passed several stations of wood. Each of the many times we passed a wooden station, you read the name of the wooden station on the building wall, moving your transparent cheeks. The echo still runs – *tap tap tap* – between the rails of my incoherence. It is already a thing of the past, but the warning signal rings louder at the crossing, and does not cease.

In a decidedly vacant stone plaza, you are tapped on the shoulder by the convulsions of a section of light, and turn back, to your delight. However, to see that the countless hidden fibers of the atmosphere were already attacking you at once and tying you up, shadow and all! Inside the convulsive laughter, fight. Because the fighting spirit is that of the enemy, flooding over the plaza.

109.   *Juglans*, with our blind eyes and ringing ears, I am the one who is eternally distraught, shorn of all I have. *Juglans,* my chest to be riven has drifted and is not here – up until the radiant station of the afterlife where anyone has relations with anyone else, it is I alone who grows bewildered, hanging between branches of migratory nerves. *Juglans,* in the radiant underground station where anyone has relations with anyone else – and I, *Juglans,* for the first time I am able to melt this rotten body in the flash of light from the one I had you keep watching for me – I dream this now.

110.   That's enough, now. I'll pass it from my lips to yours, that very special leap of a single drop in the bottle. Afterward, nut-cracking.

Nipped by what had seemed to be only a pastime, the walnut suffers. In the intricate
underpass of a certain morning, I heard a single, old-fashioned crack of thunder.
Along with the sound of the fruits of rain in the morning glow, ringing in the cupola
buried in a single stroke.   To think poems are always inducing thunderclouds
– and so what of it. Awaiting the lightning bolt that breaks open the walnut is the
lightning bolt within the walnut, as well as the elephant beetle, rove beetle, click
beetle, and your little cranium, dwelling in the folded branches.   Consumed
by thoughts of being detained from the lush disposition of death until its wrinkles
have deepened, the walnut moves along, bowing down in the void. It is a courage
that exceeds the imagination, a despair that compels the imagination. From the
sneaky lips of the clouds, finely, like a gift, the battle arrives.   The revival
of the breath upon the earth dangerously similar to the flowers' twitches of death
causes a discrepancy in the striations of the air, which quietly occurs while tearing
apart name and modifier. Leaping over time, it makes the paper bones of the cupola
decay once more into white.   Suffering stole the torturous enemy from the
walnut. But therein lies the one chance. We, too, stumble around speaking of love and
such, seek with our rooted fingers the intricate ducts of these creatures everywhere,
and with a bent tooth of light, plan to bite some off.

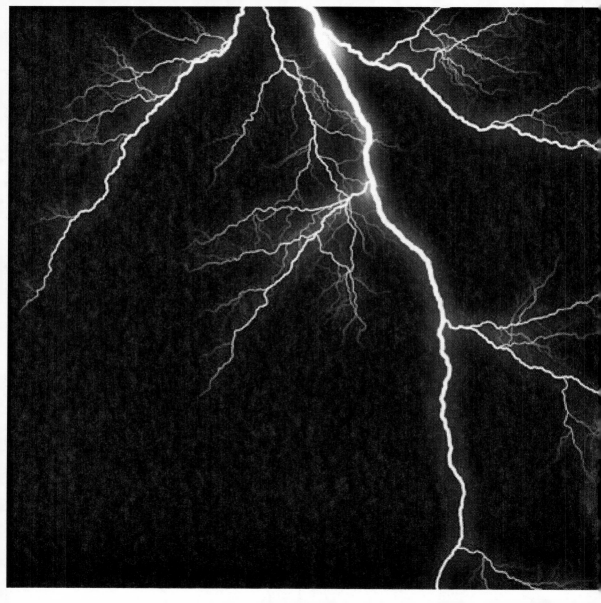

胡桃の戦意のために

胡桃の戦意のために

中保佐和子 訳

平出隆

ニュー・ディレクション・ブックス

制作地——アメリカ合衆国
ニュー・ディレクション・ブックス——中性紙使用
2008年 ニュー・ディレクション・ペーパーブック（NDP1099）として初版刊行
2008年 ペンギン・ブックス・カナダ・リミティッドにより同時刊行

Library of Congress Cataloging-in-Publication Data

Hiraide, Takashi, 1950-
[Kurumi no sen'i no tame ni. English]
For the fighting spirit of the walnut / Takashi Hiraide; translated from
the Japanese by Sawako Nakayasu.
p. cm.
ISBN 978-0-8112-1748-4 (alk. paper)
I. Nakayasu, Sawako II. Title.
PL852.I663K8 2008
895.6'15—dc22
2008000619

ニュー・ディレクション・ブックス——ニュー・ディレクション出版社により
ジェームズ・ラフリンを顕彰して出版される。
80 Eighth Avenue, New York, NY 10011

胡桃の
戦意の
ために

平出隆の『胡桃の戦意のために』の全篇が英語で出版されることはわくわくさせるような出来事である。日本語の原著が出版された一九八二年以来、この連作詩篇は二十数年間にわたって、中国語、英語、フランス語、ロシア語など、さまざまな言語に翻訳されてきた。とはいえ、そのいずれもまとまったものではなく、抜粋というかたちに留まってきた。この度、全百十一篇の英訳を集めて出版される本書の魅力のひとつは、全篇をまとめて読むことではじめて見えてくるその可能性にある。すなわち、戯れあい、乗数的に増殖し、たがいに戦いながらの主題の対位法的な展開、また、詩人の時間、胡桃の時間、日本文学史など、さまざまな時間の尺度を横切る管弦楽的な統合による包囲である。読者は胡桃をはじめ、昆虫、スモモの子、字画、視線の合う瞬間など、小さなものたちの「戦意」が、じっさいどれほど大きなものでありえ、尊厳があり、頑丈で、轟きわたるものでありうるのかに思いを致すだろう。誠実さと悪ふざけが等しく含まれる、博識の織り込まれた、この騒々しくも情愛深い作品から染み出てくるのは、感情的に高められた文学的論理の転回であり、スタイル、レトリック、構文における挑発的な運動である。そして、このとてつもなく思いやり深い詩集全体の根底にわたって、「歓声が遠くに聞える」(詩篇54)のである。するとこのことは、この本が実のところ、誰、そして何の「ために」書かれたのかを考えさせる。いま英語圏の読者は、この小さいながらも凝縮された本の「胡桃＝包み」を割り、平出隆の多岐にわたる文学的活動を、巨視的にも微視的にも検討する作業へと招待されているのである。

*

平出隆は一九六四年、十四歳のときに、敬愛するようになった数学者ヤーノス・ボヤイとニコラ

イ・イワノビッチ・ロバチェフスキーに捧げるオマージュを書き、詩人としての道を歩みだしたという。この散文的な断章を読んだ教師は「すばらしい詩である」と評して、中学二年生を驚かせた。彼には詩を書いたつもりはなかったからである。それから十二年後の一九七六年、最初にして現在まで唯一の自由詩形の詩集である『旅籠屋』の刊行によって、平出隆は戦後生まれの新世代の代表として高く評価されることになった。その成功に続く第二詩集『胡桃の戦意のために』は、大きな称賛を得ると同時に、彼のキャリアの中では早い時期の、しかし決定的な転機となったものである。

ここから平出隆は生涯をかけて、詩の理念としての散文の探究、詩的構文の拡張の探究、そして文法的な意味での「行」の詩学の探究をはじめることになる。すなわち、こうした試みにふさわしいものとして散文詩形が用いられたのである。詩的な思考と理念の種子をたっぷりと含むこの作品が、吉岡実を通じて萩原朔太郎にまで遡る日本の散文詩の系統の中に彼を位置づけて以来、平出隆は、日本の現代詩壇において最も高く評価され、最も尊敬を集める詩人の一人となった。彼の他の散文作品には、より叙述的に展開するものもあるが、『胡桃の戦意のために』においては、主要なテーマが最初の三篇にあらわれると、あとはリゾームのように、次々と継起的に展開されていく。形式は包括的であるというよりも、創発的である。木に生る果実、割られる堅果、地下から出てくる電車のように発生的なのである。

平出隆の作品をわれわれが避けがたく現代的であると感じる理由の一つは、彼の文学的な生産が狭義の意味において「詩的」であることを遥かに超えているからである。『胡桃の戦意のために』のなかには、彼が興味を示すジャンルやスタイルの多くが登場している。抒情的、現象学的、偽科学的、修辞的、抽象的、記述的、そして観察的な文体が、遊び心にあふれた巧妙なユーモアとじゃれあう。古文の語法と漢字の使用は、現代のスラングと混ぜ合わされる。なにしろこの襞の間には、日記や私記の痕跡、そして文学的な反目までもが潜んでいるのである。それでもなおこの本は、ジャンルを混淆して書く平出隆の実験の始まりに過ぎない。第三冊目の『若い整骨師の肖像』（一九八七年）では自然観察記と詩との新たな接合点が発明される一方、『家の緑閃光』（一九八四年）は自由詩と散文詩と小説的な散文とが交互に現われる形式で書かれている。二〇〇〇年、父親の死の直後に書かれた歌集『弔父百首』は、議論を

呼びながらも高く評価された。現代の詩人と歌人俳人の世界がそれぞれ、まったく分断されている日本において、平出隆はその太い境界線を超えて活動する数少ない詩人の一人である。

詩集と呼ぶことをあえてしない『左手日記例言』（一九九三年）や、シュルレアリスム的な私小説である『猫の客』（二〇〇一年）など、その他の作品では、詩とエッセイと自伝的記述とが綯い合わさっている。二〇〇二年刊行の旅行記『ベルリンの瞬間』は、詩も、フランツ・カフカ、ヴァルター・ベンヤミン、パウル・ツェランなどの旅行記の跡をたどっているが、ある章は小説とも評論とも読める。架空の国の切手を手書きで描いたアメリカの画家に宛てて書かれた『葉書でドナルド・エヴァンズに』（二〇〇一年）は、散文詩、美術論、書簡体小説あるいは日記体小説のいずれとしても捉えることができる。『ベースボールの詩学』（一九八九年）は、その名に違わず、野球に関するばかりか詩学についての本でもある。同様に『ウィリアム・ブレイクのバット』（二〇〇四年）は彼の日常生活に関する短いエッセイを集めたもので、小説家の池澤夏樹はこの本について次のように書いている。「この文章、エッセーとか随筆とか小品とか、どうもそういう名を付けたくないものなのだ。とても美しい。だがどこをどう工夫して暮らしかたが関わっているようだ。」そして言うならば、このような暮らし方こそが、詩的行為それじたいに批評的なまなざしを投げかけるのである。平出隆の批評的著作には『破船のゆくえ』（一九八二年）、『攻撃の切尖』（一九八五年）、『光の疑い』（一九九二年）、『多方通行路』（二〇〇四年）などが含まれる。より最近のプロジェクトには、明治期の詩人である伊良子清白についての画期的な評伝や、清白全集の編纂などがある。

平出隆自身は、こうした活動のすべてを冗談まじりにサボタージュと呼ぶ。というのも、数十年にわたる精力的な文学的生産を振り返りつつ、「詩人」が最後に「詩集」を出版してから二十年もの歳月が経っていることを指摘しようとするからである。彼が多くの人々から日本の現代詩人のなかで最も興味深い存在だと考えられていることや、数多くの権威ある詩やその他のジャンルの文学賞を受賞してきたことなどは、気に留めないでおこう。自身のことを（ウェブサイト上で）「日本語で詩を書いては消している者」と呼ぶ男にとっては、消去だけでなく、断片化、包摂、そして境界

という問題もまた批評的な関心の対象なのである。詩そのものからの迂回と見えるが、平出隆の詩学はそれこそがまさに要点なのである。詩壇によって定義づけられるかぎりの詩、そのような詩の確証を追い求めるより、彼は「詩形式を前提とする世界から」自身の作品を離しておくことを大切にするのである。一九九〇年代初頭に彼の作品に対して向けられた批評への応答として、平出隆は『多方通行路』で次のように書いている。「詩を離れて詩を思考することのできない人々と話をするのが苦痛になった」と。

＊

日本語の原題について読みほどいてみよう。FIGHTING SPIRIT と WALNUT は、どちらも二重の意味を持っている。WALNUT の日本語である「胡桃」は、wrapping や enclosure を意味する「包み」と同音異義語である。FIGHTING SPIRIT を意味する「戦意」もまた、fiber を意味する「繊維」と同音異義語である。したがって、本の題名には以下の意味が埋め込まれている。すなわち、「胡桃の繊維」、「包みの繊維」、「包みの戦意」である。戦いの繊維質が織り込まれ、縫い合わされ、閉じ込められ、そしてこじあけられる。最後のセクションではしかしながら、「胡桃は苦しむ」。ここで翻訳もまた苦しむことになるのだが、「詩」が、あるいは「死」が、「胡桃」に挿入されることで、ここで「苦しみ」が生まれるのである。

詩論や批評を多産するにもかかわらず、平出隆が自身の詩の背景をあらわにすることは滅多にない。煙に巻かれそうな翻訳者が刺激するときだけは例外らしいのだが。しかし、最近刊行された長篇エッセイのなかで、平出隆はこの第二詩集の一詩篇について、めずらしくみずから謎を解き明かしている。それによれば、「アーク燈の下と知らずに」とはじまる詩篇4の引用符内は、ヴァルター・ベンヤミンの『一方通行路』のなかの「アーク燈」と題されるアフォリズムだとされる。報われぬ愛に身を焦がす詩人が、会うことのできない恋人に『一方通行路』を贈った情景だとされる。贈られた女性は、「いつの日か」「アーク燈」を読みながら、それと知らずに、詩篇4自体を読むことになる、というのである。報われぬ愛のままに、こ

のようにして見えない通路が生まれる。それは遠い存在同士をつなぎ、未来と過去とをひといきに結ぶ。現実とのあいだに仕掛けられる極小の可憐な時限爆弾のように、方法としてのアナクロニズムが本をはみだし、愛によって小径をひらく。

このほかにも、アナクロニズムは言語の次元でさまざまに現われる。現代的な使用法では「妹」という言葉は「年下の女きょうだい」を意味するが、平出隆によるこの言葉の多用は、その元来の意味である、恋人もしくは年下の女きょうだいに対する情愛をこめた呼称、という用法をも含んでいる。現在の使用法では「下卑た」を意味する若者言葉である「えぐい」も、不快で苦い喉の感覚を指す本来の意味合いで用いられ、稀にしか見られない漢字の表記されるクワガタによって歌われる一節は、漢字のほかはすべて、通常では外来語を記すために使われるカタカナで綴られている(漫画などの媒体において、ロボットや外国人のしゃべる日本語の表記は、ただただしい発音の感覚を読者に与えるために、カタカナで書かれる)。本書では、カタカナとの視覚的な類似から選ばれた英語の小さな大文字が、その部分を表わすために用いられている。詩篇23においても小さな大文字が用いられるのは、古い時代の仮名遣いとともに、やはり漢字とカタカナの混淆文で書かれているからである。

平出隆の多様な語法が日本語と日本文学を垂直に縦断する一方で、彼の文学的な参照はそれと同じくらいしばしば地誌を横断する。そのなかにはブランショの「災厄のエクリチュール」や、ベンヤミンの『パサージュ論』に見られる語りへの多彩な抵抗、そして雨滴のなかの稲妻をわれわれに示すブレイク的な感受性がある。ボードレールの都市に対する不安に満ちた関係とポンジュの事物に対する偽科学的な観察が交錯させられる。同様に、断章を好むようになった経緯については、古今東西にわたる、彼が影響を受けたさまざまな名前がたどられる。断章の面白さとは「ひとつひとつの断章や断片から、他のどのひとつにつながってもいい、またつながらなくてもいい、という自由さだったろう」と彼は書く。さらにまた、詩の「行」についての研究は、「行」とそれを残す身体的行為としての筆のひとかきという物質的概念とのあいだに多義性を見いだす。そこにはわれわれに受容されている言語や詩の格付けのシステムへの問いかけがある。このような認識と関わるの

xi

だろうか、『胡桃の戦意のために』の構成については、雑誌発表時の順番をまったくくつがえして詩集内の番号に決定した。定着させるにあたって、群論の難題解決に似た数学的な経験があったといういうことが、あるとき打ち明けられている。

平出隆は『胡桃の戦意のために』を毎日の仕事で移動する電車のなかなどで制作したが、ここで電車対人間（包むもの対包まれるもの）という関係はあべこべにされる。すなわち、「その時、胸から青錆びた一軒のレールが突き出て」いくのに気づく（詩篇59）。入口と出口、内部と外部、自然と都市のあいだの対位法的な関係は、晴れやかに輝く地下鉄、あるいは故郷の潮に分け入る樹によって、いっそう明示されていく。愛と戦争との雄壮な格闘は、胡桃のスケールに投げ込まれる。ということは、暴力行為はカタツムリの固い殻において、腐りかけたスモモの子において、そして断片へと砕かれる詩行において起こるのである。実践的な野球狂としての平出隆は、詩的なダイアモンドをこのようにして満塁にさせる。そのあいだにも、ボールが人魂のように漂い、知らない者同士による視線の接触の瞬間として「ヒット」が起こる。野原や防火用水のなかでは、待機し、身構える者がいる。「すると、防火用水に若いハヤが跳ねるのだった。早く火事を、と跳ねるのだった」（詩篇92）。こうして、愛の詩における、救出のファンタジーにおける、欲せられた緊急事態における絶望的な恋い焦がれをねじ曲げるこれらの連携する断片において、現在という瞬間は増幅し拡充される——そして、あるいは、爆発させられるのである。

＊

まずはじめに、すばらしい翻訳で私を平出隆の作品に出会わせてくれたエリック・セランドに感謝したい。彼の親切な導きと日本語の詩に対する知識は、他のプロジェクトと同じくこの翻訳においても欠かすことのできない貴重なよりどころだった。翻訳の過程における手助けに関しては、さらに四谷アート・ステュディウムの中井悠、そして平出隆本人にも、感謝したい。彼らは驚くほど親切に、惜しみない忍耐、応答、訂正、提案と洞察を与えてくれた。

xii

キース・ウォルドロップには、私が文学翻訳で受けた唯一の正式な訓練について、トレーシー・グリネルには「アウフガーベ」誌における日本の現代詩特集の編集依頼について、そしてジェロルド・シロマには「デュレイション・プレス」誌に翻訳発表の場をつくってくださったことについて、それぞれ謝意を表したい。以下の人々もまた、明白なかたちで、あるいは身をもって、励ましとひらめきと力添えを与えてくれた。すなわち、ベンジャミン・バサン、ノーマ・コール、フォレスト・ガンダー、ジェン・ホファー、レイチェル・レヴィッキー、デービッド・ペリー、ローラ・シムズ、ローズマリー・ウォルドロップである。アン・ワインストックとアイリーン・バウムガートナーには、バイリンガルの装幀における見事な手捌きに謝辞を述べたい。そして最後に、ジェフリー・ヤングとバーバラ・エプラーには、この本の制作と出版すべてに関する惜しみない支援、情熱とお骨折りについて感謝を捧げる。

助成金の形ではPEN翻訳助成基金に、宿舎の形では小林茂、カン・ユージン、バード大学に、それぞれ本書の翻訳に際し物質的な支援を提供してくださった方々に感謝を捧げる。抄訳の詩篇ないしその初期形は以下の出版物に掲載されたことがある。「アウフガーベ」「カルク」「カナリウム」「サーカムフェランス」「ザ・リテラリー・レヴュー」「オクトパス」「ポエトリー」「ヴァーサル」。編集者の方々に深く御礼を申し上げる。

私はまた自分の家族にも感謝したい。ユージンが新たに加わった一家の、いつにかわらぬ愛情と支えは、私の人生と作品のほとんどあらゆる面に「翻訳」されている。

中保佐和子

晴れやかな地下鉄道。晴れ渡って涯てしない壁。日を繋いでいく轟くばかりの鋼の祈りに、ひと刷毛の雲が掛かって、はじまりよ、それがおまえの巣。

果肉の裂ける音が、きみの耳のあいだにとびちる。そのしぶきの先端は、悲哀の外にいる者に手招きしている。

降るものと、生るもの。それがぼくの関心のすべて。（降るものが生り、生るものが降りしきるまで）。生るものと、降るもの。それがぼくの欲望のすべて。（生るものがやがて生らなくなり、降るものがついに一滴も降らなくなるまで）。

アーク燈の下と知らずに、いつの日かいっしんにそのひとは読む——「報われぬ愛に身を焦がす者だけが、ひとり、その人を知る」。

格納庫の並ぶ湾岸の陽溜りに、きみは生れた。海峡ゆずりの切れ長の瞳。島々を点綴する潮の髪。灼けた頬。ときにもつれる柔かい脚。転戦にあっても、きみは声を荒げぬ技巧に死への反抗をひそませるから、その年齢はゆっくりと、日々の裏側へとどまっていく。

つむじの巻いた草叢では、朽ちた半紙や掘り出されたばかりの嘴の、柔かな破れにまぎれること。骨を折り、皮膚をひらき、それらと絡まって波打ち、消すことのできない灰汁をやがては、唇からのぼせて草の先へ、点々と滲ませるよう努めること。

硬い殻に護られて、ただ眠りゆくばかりの戦い。それは
あのいじらしい石果にとってだけではない。高層ビルの
避難階段を一列に螺旋を巻いて降りていく、果敢な蝸牛
の軍団でさえ、ひたむきに、寝息を曳いて。

氷を荷造りする思いがつづいている。なにを書き送ろう
としても、宛て名まで溶ける。届いたとしたところで、
そのひとが消えるだろう。

姦しい靴裏の星どものために、霜柱で薄化粧する道こそ
は妹。耕せば姿見ほどの扉を抜けて、自分の髪のひろが
りに逆らい、一所懸命立ちあがってくる。地底をゆく獣
が見あげるはずの、それは「狂ってる月」。

ここでは誰が内部を見透すかが、まずもって分らない。
その堅牢な膚のうえでは内部への視線がこやみなく羽化
し、その若々しくも彫りふかい皺は、外部という彫刻の
膚を暁よりもありありとさせる。渚の裂れのようにそれ
は戯れ、かつ凝固し、近づく者の失くしはじめる海のす
べてとそこに墜ちる篝星とを、どこまでもくるんでゆ
き、くるみ、そしてくるむ。

詩の形態にまつわる最終の謎は《行》ということばに棲みついている。行を分ける、行を替える。行を跨ぐ、行を渡る。行を追うごとに、行の連なりはばらばらになる。《行》は道とはいえず、環をむすぶ修練でもない。それはなにか、かけらの影だ。なにかを二重に欠く場所だ。語れよ、字画と呼ばれる切れめたち、一行の途中の行と行間。それともこれはアルキメデス・スクリュー？行為は死を食べて痩せる。

習慣の小屋に、振りおろされて斧が消える。ぼくは笑い、次に書きながら、舌は血の粒でできている、と、傍らの誰かに伝えた。板戸の隙に片眼だけでめざめる者よ、おはよう。もうはやく、おやすみ。どうせ、そこいらの枝々に胸倉を摑まれる道だよ。遠くで泣いているのは、みんなに呼び捨てにされた憧れ。アスファルトのシーツが、もう夜の皺を寄せている。

羊、牛、馬などの有蹄類の糞で巧みに丸薬をこしらえ、それを適当な場所に搬んでゆっくり食べるという奇妙な甲虫スカラボイスは、幼虫のためにはもっとも消化しやすく、もっとも営養になる羊の糞だけを選んで特殊の丸薬をこしらえます。母親はまず材料を入念に選び分け、これを細かく砕いて、地下の巣へはこびます。そして、そこで熱心な作業をはじめ、美事な梨形の丸薬ができあがると、最後まで残しておいた小さな穴から、卵を中心へ插し込むのです。やがて卵から幼虫が生れでると、彼はその巨大なる糞の塊りの中にあって、心静かに自分の周囲のものを食べながら、次第しだいに大きくなってゆくのです。

おくやみの囁かれる裏小路を、今日ぼくは三日酔いで、霞んだようになってゆっくり、ふらつく自転車を漕ぎ漕ぎ、通り過ぎていった。

靄を帯び、それでも精密に機能していくアクリル樹脂の廃墟を、西北西の崖のうえから老いた攪拌機が見下ろしている。攪拌機は記憶をほじくる、自分から無傷でありえたわずかのものたちを。花蜂、焦げしゃもじ、狂っていた磁針、百葉箱の底の水、女の舌、火。彼の仕事は終った。そして、その記憶はぼくたちの手のうちへ、いまようやくに移りつつあるのだ。

きみは、きみがはぐれつつある世界への、なおさわやかな感謝のくだもの。厳しい眠りに揺すられるための室内を、獣たちの初なつの歯が掠め、たまに首都の錆びた谿<ruby>谿<rt>たに</rt></ruby>水も横切っていく。窓として夜をひらく古いゆがんだ鏡の中で、はじまりからの無音の実、終りからの無季の雪が、肩に髪にさらにさらさら降りかかるのに、きみは気づかず、傷つかない。そのことが、触れることなくぼくを励ます。擦れ違うまま宛てのいらない感謝の果汁でぼくをみたす。扉が、扉とともにやがてこれらの幻を、埃りがちの青葉の朝へ叩き出すと知っていても。

また晴れやかな地下鉄道。まだ晴れやかな地下鉄道のあちこちに今日も、白いちいさな爆発が起る。それはぼくたちの関節の弾ける音、便利すぎた絶望が消える音。壁は落ち、地の鳥たちは巣を、日々あたらしいこの爆音の中へ仕掛けようと、いま迷うことなく搬びはじめた。

毛の生えた危険が、いつもあなたと手をつないでいますように。邪な祈りと粒よりの心配事が、つねにぼくの肺を揺すぶっていますように。そして日は流れず、愛といういうはあとわずかで確かめられず、くりかえし燃やされる物語の骨灰ばかりがぼくたちの行為を、滅びることの真実の炉へ、焚きつけていますように。

拒絶される者にもひとつかみの栄誉の灰が与えられると

いうのなら、それも捨てよう。あのひとの澄んだ悲しみ

を讃えるために。苦痛に洗われた未生の言葉はこちら岸

で、ただ朗らかにつづくばかりだ。

あそこの孤独な解体業者の猫背、あれが詩句の真の姿と

いうものじゃなかろうか。返り血のように立つ埃りにこ

とさらに素顔を隠し、壊破のあとの陽射しの強まりを、

自分のダメージであるかのごとく愉しんでいる、あの狭

い背中。

いまはかけらの形状を、苔生す無へ向けて記述すると
き。破船がいやいや翼のふりを求め、消失寸前の軒下の
消しゴムが、はじめて自分と向きあうとき、それも束の
まの幻にすぎないとき。かけらの鈍い輝きが、鋭い形状
を批判している。刃の稜線を辿る。それも素描のためで
なく、線のちぎれる瞬間に事物の汗と契約し、次なる形
へわたるために。

暗やみをおまえの胸へ、がたごとと燃えてゆく夢のレー
ルの、跡を残さない不実な認識。それはふりかかる酸素
の枝も舌で払い、ゆくてから襲うひと息きりの吹き降り
にも、色を失うことがない。まして、赤や黄の黙示にも
滞りなく。

《スベテ理論ハ、実体ヨリモチョット巨キスギルトイフ
クラヰノ暗示デスカラ、却ケルコトナク且ッ立テルコト
ナク、在リシ日ニ路頭デ唾サレタ写シ絵トシテコレニ唾
シ、丁寧ニ誠心コメテコスルベキデセウ。サスレバコス
ル指ノソノ動キニ、イッシカ絵ヨリモ、汝ノ失クシタ柔
カキ皮膚ノ方ガ描カレテクルコトデセウ。次イデソレヲ
石デ打チ、陽ニ洄ラシ、肥後守カ研イダ爪デ粗クコソゲ
テュケバ、暗示ノ粉モ小サナ嵐ヲ舞フヤウデ、マタ特別
ニ楽シイコトデセウ。》

ぼくの頭蓋のまわりをカフカフと、律儀な鴉がめぐって
いる。鴉よ、鴉、千駄ヶ谷の、浅い森の、人情篤いハシ
ブトガラス。敵対する友よ。

汽車を降りると、出口は北へのひとつしかなかった。酒
屋と乾物屋と米屋くらいがくりかえし並ぶ印象の、線路
沿いの古くおとなしい商店街を抜け、つまりは長い駅舎
をぐるり南へと迂回した。案内の人をえてようやく、私
は憧れの木の前に立つことができるのだった。

沈黙の手の中で生きものへと変身する石鹸。死に近づく
者の爪跡が香りたかく肌に泡立つ、その鉄道。

誰が猶予と見ようとも、ぼくはだんだん苦しくなる。右
手の甲を縦にひらいて、塩鹹い古着の天気を呼び入れ
る。海との際から崩れるやつを。そして血管を、きつい
繊維の草で結ぶ。

打撃にはまだつめたい澄んだ陽溜りをゆく。河川敷では
それでも、口々になにか叫びながら石で、廃車を打ち据
えている少年たち。

やっぱり渦を巻きはじめた。ゆくてから寄せる指令に、揺れているあのキールの突端を見てごらん。記憶のまっさらを透かしてごらん。結ばれて、ゆくえを告げる鈴が舞い、舞う鈴の中、ほら、やっぱり渦が巻きはじめた。

敷石に滲む血漿。締めあげてくる逞しい腕。この都市の濁った光りは、おもむろにぼくを組み伏せ、打ち据え、ばらばらにする。ぼくは霞む眉間にひろがる七月の工事現場。ぼくは殴りかかる。鐵苦茶の晴れ間に。その中心にいる誰かに。誰のでもない涙があふれて、舗石に窪んだ鳩尾を、打つように洗いはじめる。

打撃するものが不足していく。打撃せよ。垂直に樹木を抱え、ゆっくりと天に突きあげ（青にめまいし）、静かに胸もとまで下ろしてきたら、力を抜いて身構えているろ。一条の気配の稲妻が木目を伝って降りてくる。野のむこうからは拳ほどの人魂が、ゆるゆるとカーヴを描いて炎えてくる。一瞬しなって、打撃せよ。打撃するものが不足していく。打撃せよ。

翼を脱ごうとするコムクドリの汗を、はばたく舌でどうして、ぬぐってあげない。水くさいよ、街はずれの樹上の恋びと。古着屋の吊るしの蔭から、羚羊がひとりきみを見ている。鉄色の侮蔑の瞳。

révolution… 　旅籠はきょう無限のオルガン。わたくし
は分断する、そのつましいカノンを。わたくしは抑圧す
る、逃げまどう嬰へを、沈んだままのタイを。わたくし
はわたくしが統治する旋律を再分解する。わたくしは、
わたくしが鎮圧する律動でふるえるわたくしを、再破砕
する。しかるのちその抑圧を分断を分解を破砕を、百十
一の偽の終止で再統制する。なぜ? わたくしもまた力
のかけら。事物の権力にすぎないからだ。これについて
は、別のかけらも触れるだろう。

難破する光り。割れた唇をさらに大きくひらき、髪を銹
びつかせた海をおまえは呼び込む。泡沫と涯てばかりで
つくられた献身の街へ、一月の黒馬の息で乗りあげると
きにも。七つの灘に崩れる胸、水の布として一気に、ひ
きちぎられる宙。いま人間はその瞬時の裂け目、応える
ものをもたぬ、彼方の影にすぎない。だが、見ろ。難破
し、捩じられる光りの端よ。砂粒をつけたおまえの踵の
膝が、跳躍の青褪めた収縮に耐えはじめたさまを。侮蔑
の、打擲の、草の香りの立ち昇る中に。

「この先難所あります」

残暑お見舞。やどり木と戦って暮した夏休みも、遅刻すれすれに逝ってしまった。窓辺ではどうしても言葉の未来へ想像が過ぎるので、頬杖で、想像への嫉妬を叩いています。この街の感情も言語のパルスに過ぎません。早い朽ち葉を送りました。では、きみのキ印の燔祭まで。

かつては果肉の瑞々しい繊維によって戯れのまま走らされた網の目状の通路が、いまそのまま、全体をこれ以上にない堅さで被うに至る——、この完璧の鈴をふれ。われわれの、裸火厳禁の地下道に、このすっかり晒された迷路をふれ。最初、それは鳴らない。最初、それは鳴らない。

もう一度言ってみろ、もう一度。もう一度言ったらどんな砂が舞うというのか試しにここで、おい、もう一度言ってみろ。

周縁の稀薄さを主題にして、成就しなかったもののかた
ちを見極めること。たとえば、わたしの亡骸を覆いはじ
めていく風のかさぶた。そのあえかな細胞を出入りし、
息づかせてもいる、懲りない誕生への欲望の音楽。

逆光の都市の尾根筋を辿って、脈絡の要所で湧き水を呑
む。部屋に入り、色刷り新聞に胸を崩したところで、脈
を測る。こうして今日も、詩の一行はおまえを撃たず、
長い迂回路の、夕闇に包まれはじめてようやく浮きでる
音もなく水っぽい一部分にすぎない。だが、腸壁の鈍い
輝きももつ道を微速の弾丸の気持ちを曳いてすすむこと
も、また格別の試煉には違いない。

錐もむ岬の、はだらのたてがみにしがみついて冬波の夜
へ、流れる鬪を過ぎた。日は落ち、燈台なお暗く眠りこ
み、海一面で風が錫に吹き変わった。ときすでに遅くぼ
くは見た、つくばって抱く土の舳先の海へ躍る内部
に、潮さびた地下鉄道が眼差しよりまっすぐに轟いてゆ
くのを。その最後尾には、背に緑のヒトデをつけたぼく
の死んだ人たち…

観念の発生をゼロへ、おしつめていくと白い爆発があ
る。それを、それだけを詩と、呼びたい気持ちにぼくは
傾く。日射しにまぎれるほどの不幸を、崖下の円屋根の
下で幾度か浴びた。あいあいと頭に、雨の実の生るあい
だに。

蜘蛛は天才である。季節をつなぐ雲よりもさらに高い大気の層を気団を率い移動する神速。蜘蛛は天才である。降下十六方への燦きは重力を逃れるパラシュートでなく、空全体に筋を与え、光りの雫を地へみちびく。ついでに自分を降ろすにすぎない。あんなに透きとおる骨、折れてもあふれる骨があるだろうか。しかも彼は種子。忍耐と想像を滋養として、策謀はむしろ無。おのれをふくむ、誰の栄光も認めない軽やかな邪悪。蜘蛛はただの天才である。

詩句は被分断を力としている。未来にも過去にも頼らず、行間と行間のあいだをひたすらに懸垂している。たったひとりで闇の中で、長く泣きつづける子供のように、みずからを時の影からどこまでも引き離そうとしている。しかも、そんなものたちが、分断を介して連なっているのだ。

内角へ沈む光りに、愛用の黒バットを折ってしまった。

すると東京湾第13号埋立地小球場はうらうらの左打席を中心に芝を消して、波がしらがささめくようにそよいでくる。いいよ。いつまでも笑ってくれよ。かつて見つめた折れ口どもを記憶の宙へ、解けた筏のようにあつめはじめた、年齢も後悔もない素手の打ち手を。

色づく果樹園の果樹にまぎれ、憧れはいかにもわが構想の杜撰さにふさわしく、虫どもに喰いちぎられた葉となって目前に繁り、反対に彼の萎えきった敵意がこちらの身うちに、確然としかも無防備に閉じられていくようだった。

自分の外に美しい影を認めて、生きものは傷つく、胸の
あたりで。触れようとして伸べられた苔生す手は、失う
ことを恐れ、まだ宙に引攣っている。けれども、告げる
声なく　告げなければならない。呼吸は　もう小さな嵐、
と。いとしいものには、生きものの破綻を懸けて。

いくつもの袋小路を発見していく仕事。辛抱づよく、実
地に歩いて。見つけたらすぐに、口を縛る。都市の秘部
で、袋同士に針穴ほどの息のかよい路ができるのを、た
だひたすらに待つ。破裂・連鎖。あとには、紐をといて
歩くさわやかな仕事が残されているだけ。

暮れていく駐車場脇の、申し訳程度の草叢で、ノコギリクワガタムシが黙って歌う。「ボクノ愛シカタハこめつきョリ劣ル。歩キカタハぞうむしニモ及バナイシ。コノ歌イカタモ、はねかくしノョリハルカニハズレル。ソレデモマダ、藪イ茎ヲ噛ミシメ、ソコイラジュウヲボクハ飛ビ廻ル。ソレハ、ボクノ存在ニイツカシカタナク賛成スル、ソノひとノ過チヲ信ジテイルカラ」

清潔な犯行を追い立てに掛かろう。

路面の氷雪をぎりぎり軋いてこの場を離れる自転車の、

崩れが次々と起り、光線が縦にそそぐと、ぼくの出番。

よ、ぼくはおまえの息だ。あちこちの樹の枝で小さな雪

主（あるじ）なく吊りあげられていく床を、虫の息で匍い過ぎる者

どんな拒絶の詩学によっても、比喩をとおして睦みあうもの同士の**歓び**は隠しきれまい。**超高層ビル**の屋上近い北壁に、シロツメクサの花粉がひとつぶ食いこんでいるのは、見ようとすれば見ることのできる、ささやかな**修辞**の眺めだ。天気雨に打たれつづける彼らの語らいを読むといい。「**読者を拒み**」はじめる、その高い高い濡れ場まで。

タクシーの闇から、彗星をうかがう悪い**癖**。そう、その先の死んだ信号を左へ、ハンドルいっぱいに、突き当りの時計店のウィンドウを掠って右へ。やがて尾っぽくらいは曳いて、下へ。晴れやかな地下鉄道へ。

風は車輛を抜け、青いシートの陽溜りは移らず、ぼくは死線にあえぐひとに会いにいく途中だ。ゆきあった優しいものと途中まで、遊びのように視線を交わし、立ちあがり、別れ、電車の後尾へ風とともに歩いていく。おお、進行方向を忘れる。終りの窓からひらけていく新緑の首都。窓の終りよ。病院から、笑みさえ浮べ、ぼくはまた戻ってくるのだろうが。

ふかい屑物入れの暗がりの中途で、スモモの子はようやくにめざめた。「ああ、ぼくは、跳ぶこともなく、硬く光るものも知らずに腐るよ」。それから、濡れた包装紙やパン屑のあいだを、自分二箇分ほど下へずり落ちた。

歓声が遠くに聞える。

語が手をつなぎあってつくる 最初の虚構からぼくが来た。ぼくは物語を最小限に切詰める者、絡みあっている語の指たちを、仕返しの一行で切っては歩く者だ。この人知れぬ散歩には、見通しも帰りも、お情けもない。

きみの腕が、捩じれたレールになって、錆びて延びているよ。きみの脇の斜面に、草の実がひとつ、轢かれて潰れているよ。踵は傷つき、白い煙りがあふれているよ。おれは助けられない。きみの、ひかがみから白い煙りが、ひどく立っているよ。

緑の皮にくるまれた魂。密生するひとつひとつに、雷雨の雫がぶらさがってる！

その影といると、霧雨の帷りを分けて危ない方へ、どこまでもどこまでも歩いてゆける気がした。もう瀝青の花はだらしなく崩れて落ち、塀という塀はふやけてふるえていた。自分の胸から指を抜くと、私は思い切ってその手をとって、ふたりながら宙へらあと意味なく翻ろうとした。だが、それよりはやく降りはじめた雨の実の、道を打つ音よりなおはやく、閃光がすべての跳躍を打ち消していた。

その時、胸から青錆びた一軌のレールが突き出て、目の前のアスファルトへ降りていくのに気づいた。着地に合わせて膝をつくとさらに速くそれは延びて、前方にぽつんと薄黒い石の建築の、腹部にひっそり抱えているというふうの地下への階段に吸い込まれた。軌道を胸へたぐり戻すようにして匍いながら、やっとのことで入口に辿りつき、中を覗く。骨で組まれた空洞の遙かむこう、二本の光りが交わるあたりに、鈍く翳るもの。そして、いつからか高鳴ってくるもの。

実現と現実の、ふたつの熾りのあいだのかくも不自然な旅程。行為の宿は弱まり果てた野火に呑まれ、逃げはじめる唸りが行為する。このいじましい羽撃きと静止も、ついにはぼくたちのものだ。傍点のようにつきまとうこの蠅としての現実を、自分の声の裏にも装えぬ者は、局面と局面とのあいだに、すでに叩き潰された胡麻の灰だ。

ぼくの小学校の黒板に、ビスで留められていた接ぎだらけの翼。輪転機から刷り出されてきた半熟の夕陽。つやつやと靡く同級生の手脚を分けて、鉱物の沈黙のおしえだけ守り、川底の標本室の窓を蹴破ってぼくは、おお卒業した月の繊い夜、単独で、硬い消しゴム一ケ持って。

颱風が、逝く夏を組み伏せつつ近づき、波が堤の小家を洗い、燈が断たれると、書斎の天井に貼りつけておいた地図の湾に懐中電燈の鈍い円をあて暉造は、沈黙に船を棄て海村に晩年を休む不機嫌の伊良子清白は、豹変して嬉々となり「いまに 風向きが 変りはじめるぞ」「このまま北上か、右旋回」と、気象学書二巻を傍らに熱狂を帯び、ぐらついて、胸を揺すったという。その小舟。

眼差しは、長すぎるからすぐにつかまる。つぶらな湖へ注いで、ひどくしぶく。しぶきをつなぐ振り返った眼差しと、一瞬の間もなく絡みあう。道と道とが交わるように、自他を失くすまで睦みあう。憎しみの冬、蔑みの夜、決然とした拒絶の丘の朝にさえも。長すぎる意味の糸がほつれて、失神の沖が青くひろがる。ひとりの瞳を見る者は、もう、すべての水への溺死者。

胡桃を綺麗にふたつ割りする不思議な小動物の形跡にかんする民間からの黄ばんだ報告をわたしが読んだのは、胡桃の花盛りを分けてすすむ古い列車に乗って死ぬ人のいる故郷へと帰っていった黒髪ながい女性からのいかにも手短の便りを手にした同じ晴れ渡った午後でしたが、その萌黄の葉書はわたしの一日の小屋の昏れ方をまさにふたつ割りして届いたのでした。

わたしがつねに交信しているものは、高い樹冠に結ばれたプリズムの中の腕。その肱のあたりに烟る虹。どんな微細な生きものからも、言葉はとどいているらしい。それがしかも、日に打ち据えられる樹間の鈴生り、燃えるモビールに連なっている。経験の饐えた水をつかって、遠い路傍で、わたしもまた貧しい影を組み立てる。

だからまた、詩句はこなごなの支配。そんなことにさえ忌避するばかりで過ごす神経は、この薄墨の懸崖を立ち去るがいい。かけらは触れる手を切るだろう。

森永ミルクキャラメル一箱買って、破片の詰った頭陀袋を抱えて、総武・中央線各駅停車は空高く首都を東西に横切る。これはぼくの書斎です。人語駅ごとに退いてみち、津田沼あたりで折り返せば、靴裏はざらざら。冬の夕闇が誘うように青く澄み、迷っていた眼差しも紙の奥からゴトトゴトンと折り返します。眼をこすれ。たくさんの窓と扉と吊り革をもつ（網棚もある）、ベルが鳴り笛が鳴る、ここは死んだ信号士の子の書斎です。

いくつもの夏を過ぎて、ある詩人はこう書きとめた──「失われたものから なぜ 学ぶことになるのだろう」。底冷えの線路際の暗闇で、悪い酔いにまだ傾いて、せめて一日の終ることを希いながらいつかぼくは、おかしな思いをつないでいる──失っていくものから、いま学ぶことはできるだろうか。

（こんなところに転がっていても、砲弾に負傷し、繃帯を巻かれた、ギョーム゠アポリネール゠アルベール゠ウラジミール゠アレクサンドル゠アポリネール・コストロヴィツキーの恋する大きな頭部について、ぼくは片時だって忘れたことがない）。

ひとつ投げてくれないかい、微塵の詩句が唯一の武器であるときに、梁のうえで初めのせせらぎに休息する野兎さん、そこから、ことばをひとつ……すると、「一撃」。

黴びたアルミフォイルに音響がとびちる。

崩れる気象を追うことを予報図から諦めるのは、おまえもまた生きものであるためだ、とぼくは思う。葉叢から発し、春の羽虫のように宙にみち、樹肌のぬくみを求めては萎びる。腐臭が追うだろう。木の下水から下水道へ、論理は分れ、像はこぼれる。だが

まったく、ここまで来て。ひどいったらないよね、お互い。書かれた限りのことさえ読めないんだから。読まれる限りのことさえ書けないんだから。この世の、紙という紙、肉という肉に浅くとり憑いた屈折率。鏡への手紙、ブリキの日記、……波のうえに幾度も消したただひとつの名。絶望？　いやいや。水平線を栞りにして、青空をここへ閉じるばかり。

蟷螂の絶える穴を抜けでると、もうたとえばの話は終っていた。風の蔭にまわったところを露営地とし、ここから、希望と石榴の腐敗を、石榴と銃口の密会を、すべてひと連なりに眺めるとしよう。逐次の観察が風の骨組になり、風が自分の首根っ子を、知らずに摑んで揺すぶって吹くまで。

洪水も木霊も、ウレタンと下水道に吸われて終る。遠くの窓から途切れがちにピアノ、窓の近くは若いケヤキのざわざわ。それらもやがて、燃える鼓膜に吸われたままで終るだろう。人混みに呑まれてもうみえないひとよ、ぼくは元気だ。洪水も木霊もなく、しごく元気だ。

星屑、太陽、土星、雷光。白や橙の数字や記号に穢れて
いるばかりではない。ある見方に従えば、道は宇宙的で
また性的な接ぎあてにみちている。ガス、水道、電話、
電力、警察。警察? マンホールから耳だけ出している
兎を、だんだんに見掛けなくなった。

身を刻る希望に堪えたあとやすやすと列車に乗って、樹
は樹自身を訪れる。海へ垂れていく萎びた穂状の街並
を、それでも生きものの尾のように辿りそのまま、ふる
さとの潮に分け入る。過ちだとは知れたことさ。父よ、
葉先の。ことばはみな花後ノ石果。

わたくしはもう永く、破片を整理しつづけている。手提げ袋いっぱいの袋小路のそれぞれを、より余裕ない形に追いつめ、互いが通じあわないうちにまた偶然の陳列ベルトに委ねている。この仕事は長びけば長びくほど、破片から破片へと渡る手を、破片にひとしい一中間項と変える。

リスは、すなわち木鼠です。地上へも来ますが、多くは樹のうえをまわり歩いて、植物質を荒します。リスの食わない樹の実は少ないくらいでしょう。ことにブナ、カシ、クルミの果実は、ひどくわたしの好むところであります。

敵のふところにかき抱かれたままでいていまさら、どんな恋文が声明が遺言が、あるというのか。われわれはみな、内側に刺草の野を包んだ不発弾だ。へだてる愛しいもの同士をもたぬ隔壁だ。肩に掛かったセロファンの裂れに皺だらけの眼が映っている。必ず、正確な断面で壊れる物たち。奴らと、いまはその断面をとおして別れるときだ。

思い出の抽斗にも未来の棺桶にもいないぼくの息子よ、聴け。もはやおまえは、露地に捨てられ、口をこぼたれ、絵柄までやくさにかすれた楽器のように、小さなうろになけなしの風を起し、自力でふるえて、晴れていくよりないのだぞ。うずくまるひと裂れを励まし、ゆきずりのひと裂れに慰められ、そうしておのずと綴れあわさる旋律に自分を支え、そうしておのずと立ってくる戦慄に自分を変えていくよりほかに、さあ、もうどうやら術はないのだぞ。

腐葉土のひろがる空を踏切士は眺めよ。そこをでたらめに通過する枯れた稲妻、土龍の骨格、船酔いの幻の類いに、鳴り響いて果てたばかりの片腕をおもむろに挙げよ。石綿の帽子は目深くしていよ。地中の待機は裏切りの、やがてシグナルにみちる。

接骨院のふやけていびつな角を曲る、ああまがるよ。風は青い漿液と変わり、吹かずふるえ、雲のブロックは膨らんでは縮む。沸き立つ胸のうえでみだりに、指がひらくよ。みだりにひらくよ。

日本橋高島屋の一階西寄りから二階へ向うエスカレータ
ーのうえで、ある日、雨後の午後、一匹の蝸牛を目の前
にしてぼくは、その韻の踏み具合の無意味に思わず深く
嘆息したものだった。彼は屋上の緑へ赴くのか、それと
も大食堂の調理場へ直行か。やはりなにか、買物がある
のか。せめて奇術コーナーまでは高まれよ、渦巻き。小
声で励ましたが、照れたようにちょっと、ツノをひくつ
かせたとしかみえなかった。

遠くからの響きだけで守られた厳密な部屋。そこでの内
省と惑乱──*Juglans*──惑乱と祈り──*Juglandaceae*
──自分を小動物と考えても救いではない。

場末の「中華」の染抜きの下の、生きるための戸惑い。
食品見本のウィンドウに映って、人だかりが揺れている。偶然に寄り合いそれぞれに、癒すものと癒されるものの実質を、想像の秤に掛けている。そんな死後の夕暮れの中。

詩は、人が思うものとあまりに違いつづけてきた。そうに違いない、と思ういま、居酒屋の棚が傾く。

羽蟻を潰すときいっそう細い指先の、闇雲のうごき。誤

字を消すときいっそう太くぐちゃぐちゃと湧く、黒雲の

筆跡。おれが死ぬとき、ほんとうの雲間から、どんな鳥

が胸もとへ降り立ち、どんな錯乱の爪跡を残して、絶え

絶えの魂を啄むだろう。

もし作品が世界の災厄から難をまぬかれ、同時にその災

厄を自己の世界の酸素としても包み込むことができたな

らば、手をつなぎあっているとみえる語と語、その息と

息、気配と気配とのあいだの間隙こそがその堅牢の基な

のである。この虚ろな穴を中継して、作品は世界へと裏

返される。そしてわれわれは、作品のひとつひとつの風

穴を、作家の時間をくつがえしつつ順不同に読むという

最終的な権利、作品に対して、いわば最後の災厄を行使

する権利をもつ者である。

最も大切に思うものによって、轢断されていく魂。だが轢断が、それを轢断の理由としたとおり、彼は待っていたのかもしれない。自分の残骸を。その飛散を。最後の轟きの中でふるえる胡桃の、懸命にこちらへ向かってうずくのを、たしかにぼくは見たような気がする。

冷えた瞳のひろがりに飛び交う、草の生えたコンクリート・ブロック。運河を蔽って立ち並ぶ千の柩のそれぞれには、さらに千の冷えた瞳。その懸崖を駆け降りる霧の子の旅団。一挙に死都を編みあげる無限の反射。これほどの幻惑の中でなら秘術をつくして、妹よ、いつまでもいつでも、いないおまえを抱き締めることができる。

借景の樹間を抜けてきた若いそよぎが、窓ガラス越し、自分を移動性高気圧だと言い張っている。陽気な詐欺師め。腕力の春、衰える暈と湧く光りとの均衡を確かめることに、おまえは疲れた。ぼくもまた、身うちに湧くものが正午の天秤を費してしまったのを、その嗄れ声に、すばやく知るのだ。

すると、防火用水に若いハヤが跳ねるのだった。早く火事を、と跳ねるのだった。

カイとかいう名を推定される古代エジプトの書記官の遺
像の、パピルスを左の掌に胸を張って坐した類型的なポ
ーズは、口述する王の言葉の脈絡・変容すべてへの全身
これ耳または手となる注意であったことを示す以上に、
彼の第一等級の職業、職業を超えた職業についての誇り
にみちた忘却でもあった。しかし今日、右の手に葦のペ
ン（と推定されるもの）は失われ、各部位にはわずか
つの破損と博物館的至福さえ染みついている。

Juglans　めしいと耳鳴りの中で、　荒れた時間の涯ての
その角を曲ろう。　*Juglans*　交接と洪水の兆しの中で、
胸を打ち棄て、また打ち棄て、あげられるだけの声を荒
げて、殺伐とした日の涯てのその階段を降りてゆこう。
季節は破れた。そして雲が波が、　羞じらいながら地に狂
おしくみち、*Juglans*　晴れやかな偽の死後が、ゆっく
りとわれらの地下をめぐりはじめる。

詩形式の戦いは、舗道に投げおかれた雑巾のように、零れたばかりの星々に濡れている。そのうえを通過するものは通過するためだけの機械であり、無視するためだけの一瞥である。定型的陣営はこういう景色の浮きあがる一角に盲目でありつづけているが、古い掛け声に包まれているのはむしろ、詩形式の自由をもってぐるりの舗石を転覆せんと息巻く尖端病者たちのひと句切りだ。彼らは、自由詩形式とはすでに権力の自在の形式であり、雑巾もまた国旗のように翻るのであることに、小さな眼を閉じる。

快心の打撃だけが悲しみのゆくてを教えてくれて、痛烈な光りだけが、崩れた胸を慰めにくる。土のしぶきのひとつひとつが、待ちわびた終りにふるえているし。感謝とともにこの場所を、澄み切った空へくつがえそうか。

消されてそこにあることの至福。砕かれてその形で、最初の光りを浴びる歓び。水打たれた痕跡が零度の火事にびちびち狂い、結晶する力を壊す力へ、壊す力を壊れる物のふためきへ、いま生きた渦の過程に打ち返す。

くるみ、そこはひどい目に遭うよ。どうしてそんなとこ
ろに、黒い汗にまみれて。くるみ、ぼくたちは近づいて
いる。聞えないか、ぼくの鋼の轟き。

百十一の各車輌が同時に、白夜の稀薄な先頭を切る列車。その連結は任意。百十一の各車輌がすべて、背後に萎びた風景を棚びかせる列車。その解体は随意。こんな列車の走る軌道はいかなるものか、列車よ、幻のこの場をかりて、図示せよ。

最後の力をふるい起してぼくは、きみの青褪めた戸口へプレゼントしよう。別の瞳へ向うための、最初の食べものとなるように。封印された渦潮。繃帯もあらたな太陽。智恵ある石果。

毀れたばかりの甕の中で揺れる、騒乱の水のつめたさ。不運に祝福されて、わたしたちは離れる。むかし、川がそうしたように。むかし、人間がそうしたように。疲れた風はさらに疲れた方がいいのだし、色褪せた葉叢はさらに色褪せた方がいい。ちぢこまってしまった魂は、たくさんのつぶてとなって散らばればいい。いつか、わたしの祝福するとびきりの不運が誰のものか、敵たちも、恋人たちも、不意に芽吹く朽ち木のもとで、にがく知るだろう。

妹。それは内縁の稲妻、地下道を抜けるちぎれ雲。胸の奥の遠火事、光りでできた鍵穴。もっとも冷静なもっとも辛辣な、真珠。

窓はいつも、小さな墓地を見つめている鏡だった。あやふやな視線によってそこを耕しているばかりの日々というものが、誰にもある。あやふやな鉄の手摺りを伝った木の家の二階のひと部屋が、もちろんぼくにも昔あった。

手のひらに包まれ、水が熟れる。それでも水が崩れないのは中で、花が身を捩っているそのせいか。力は昏れ、美も状態にすぎない。見つめず、飲み干さず、高塔のように、あの日の高塔の緑のたてがみのように、自分を木霊ない恋情の底に、立たせたい。投身の気絶のままに、靡かせたい。岸のない湾をそこない。

階段を降りてゆく霧の詩法も、ここまで恋がこころにみちてようやく、蛇と旋律を繋いだ。とうに暴かれていた秘蹟と、はばたく無知なセキレイ一羽とを、希望の裏に折りあわした。切立つのどの壁から、躍るよう、群青の錆が白紙のうえにあふれている。身を焦がす言葉、その枯れた骨たちの浅く繁る地底に、わたしの影はふたたび立ち、しかしここがどんな野への、もう鍵穴となるわけでもない。

なんと多くの失敗が、それと知れぬまま、日々われわれに打ち寄せるのだろう。にがい波になってこみあげてくるシグナルとともに、だんだんに分ってくる教えがある。けれどもその蔭には、だんだんに怪しくなっていく真実がある。

いくつもの木の駅を過ぎた。いくつもの木の駅を過ぎる

たび、透ける頬をうごかしてあなたは、木の駅の名を駅

舎に読んだ。わたしの支離滅裂のレールのあいだを、と

んとんとと、その木霊はまだ駆けている。もう事後な

のに、踏切警報機がさらに高く鳴ってやまない。

空虚と見るほかなかった石の広場で、一筋の光りの痙攣

に肩を叩かれ、振り返っておまえは歓ぶ。けれど、もう

そのとき、隠れていたおびただしい大気の繊維が一挙に

おまえに襲いかかり、影もろともに縛りあげていると

は。痙攣する笑いの中で、戦え。戦意は敵のものだか

ら、広場をあふれて。

Juglans めしいと耳鳴りの中で、身ぐるみ剝がれ、永遠にとり乱すのはわたしだ。*Juglans* 掻き毟るべき胸も流れてここにはなく、晴れやかな、誰もがだれもと交わるという死後の駅まで、この移動性の神経の樹間に吊りさがって乱れていくのは、ひとりわたしだ。*Juglans* 晴れやかな、誰もがだれもと交わりあう地底の駅で、そしてわたしは、*Juglans* おまえが見つめつづけてくれたあのひとの閃光にはじめて、腐れたこの身を溶かすことができるのだと、いま夢みる。

もう充分だ。きみに口移ししよう、とっておきの、壜の中の一滴の飛躍。そのあとで、くるみ割りだ。

慰みと考えていたものに歯を立てられて、くるみはくる
しむ。入りくんだある朝の地下道で、ぼくは古臭い雷鳴
をひとつ聴いた。一撃で埋められた円屋根に鳴る朝焼け
た雨の実の音も。　　　いつでも詩篇たちが雷雲を
立てていると思うのはどうだろうか。くるみを割る稲妻
を待っているのはくるみの中の稲妻であり、その畳まれ
た枝に棲むゾウムシやハネカクシ、コメツキ、そしてお
まえの小さな頭蓋だ。　　　みずみずしい死の配列
から歔ふかくなるまで弾かれてあることを、考えつめ真
空にうなだれて、くるみは移動している。それは想像を
絶する勇気、想像を強いる絶望。ずるがしこい雲の唇か
ら繊く、贈り物のように戦いがとどく。　　　草花
の死のひきつりに危うく似たその息の地上での蘇りは、
空気の筋をたがえさせ、名と形容とを裂きながら静かに
起る。時を跳び、あの円屋根の紙の骨を、それはもう一
度白く朽ちさす。　　　くるしみはくるします敵を
くるみから奪った。だが、それが好機なのだ。ぼくたち
も、愛などと言いあいながら転び、そこらじゅうの生き
ものの入りくんだ管を根の指で探し出し、折れ曲った光
りの歯で、喰いちぎる気だ。